A Deacon On Purpose

Four Biblical Essentials

Second Edition

Dr. Tony Wolfe

A Deacon on Purpose: Four Biblical Essentials

Second Edition © 2024 Tony Wolfe

Cover Art: Hunter Sample

ISBN 978-1-955295-42-0

Requests for information or permissions should be addressed to:

COURIER PUBLISHING

100 Manly Street
Greenville, South Carolina 29601
CourierPublishing.com

PUBLISHED IN THE UNITED STATES OF AMERICA

*This book is dedicated to countless devoted
deacons who serve Christ's churches with refreshing
faithfulness and determination.*

Foreword

The church needs deacons who know why they were selected, what they are called to do, and how they can effectively fulfill God's calling. The church needs deacons on purpose. If you're a deacon seeking to fulfill your purpose, you've chosen a great resource.

When the first edition of *A Deacon on Purpose* was released, it was an instant blessing from God in my role as editor of Lifeway's *Deacon Magazine*. It was also a great asset in my work with the Hawaii Pacific Baptist Convention. The book was a natural fit to feature in the magazine. It gave me countless ideas for subjects, and I asked Tony to write for almost every edition of *Deacon Magazine* since the book was released. Tony has included some of his best magazine articles in the appendix at the back of this second edition.

In serving our convention of churches in Hawaii, the Pacific, and Asia, *A Deacon on Purpose* became a staple for buying in bulk and giving to every pastor and deacon I encountered. It formed the content for the trainings I led for deacons. I've taught the content of this book to pastors and deacons in Hawaii, Japan, and The Philippines. Every group found it relevant to their situation.

I am honored to introduce you to the revised and expanded edition. Tony Wolfe has taken his excellent work and updated and elevated its usefulness to an even greater degree. The world has changed significantly since Tony released the first edition, and while the purpose of deacons has stayed the same, the need for deacons on purpose is greater now than ever.

This book is biblical, practical, and easy to comprehend. It includes four easy-to-digest chapters on the four purposes of a deacon, a chapter of introduction, and a final chapter on the deacon's character qualities and qualifications. You can read the entire work in two to three hours. The book's format lends itself to either one-time or ongoing training for deacon bodies or for groups of deacon bodies from churches in the same region.

Invite another pastor or denominational leader to lead an all-day retreat that offers an overview of the book. When your deacon fellowship meets, discuss a chapter or a portion of a chapter using the provided discussion questions. Give a copy of this practical resource to every deacon who serves your church. When new deacons join your fellowship each year, give them a copy and revisit the training.

Thank you, Tony, on behalf of countless pastors and deacons who have been blessed by this book and those who will be blessed by this revised and expanded edition.

Dr. Craig Webb
Executive Director-Treasurer
Hawaii Pacific Baptist Convention
General Editor, *Deacon Magazine*
2024

Original Foreword

Everyone knows *who* a deacon is. But most people, including the deacon himself, may not know *what* he is! To define what it means to be a deacon requires looking no further than the Greek word that is translated "deacon" in the New Testament. The word itself tells us what a deacon is. He is a "servant," willing to do whatever is necessary to advance the cause of Christ and the witness and unity of the church. The word itself does not speak of personal authority or personal recognition. It describes a person whose life is totally committed to the Lord Jesus Christ and his church. He is a person who stands tall to set the example for what a genuine believer should be. He is loyal to the Lord, to the church, and to his pastor and staff. He is the indispensable ingredient in keeping a church moving forward toward the high purpose for which our Lord established the church. He is the man who always stands with the pastor, determined to protect the pastor's time so he can truly hear from God and always have a word from God when he stands to preach. He is the guardian of the unity of the church. He is the spearhead of the mission of the church. Without his loyalty and sterling integrity standing prominently for God to always be glorified and praised through the church, the church will likely flounder in its focus on our great, creative, redemptive God.

Sounds like he is indispensable to the church and to the pastor and staff, doesn't it? Truthfully, he is! The deacons arose out of the need to protect the time of the Apostles from necessary and important things that had become an increasing burden to them. The enemy of the best is not the worst, but the good. Good and needed things can absorb the energies and passion of God's undershepherds. That happened in the early church. The deacons were called into being in the early church for the purpose of freeing up the Apostles to spend more time in prayer and in hearing from God so they could proclaim God's truth to the church. The same need is present today. A thousand important things can overwhelm the pastor so that he does not have the energy or time to truly hear from God. The deacon was God's provision to be a friend, counselor, support and encourager to the pastor. In that role, he stands to serve in any needed way to strengthen the ability of the pastor to spend more time in prayer and study to always declare God's Word with clarity and application.

I thank God as I look back over my decades of ministry for the deacons God brought into my life. They fulfilled in every way the description Tony Wolfe has given of deacons on purpose. These pages are not rocket science, just simple explanations of the biblical role of the deacon as the one who frees up the pastor to fulfill his ministry that God has given to him. Read them with great benefit. Apply these principles with great blessing!

Dr. Jimmy Draper
President Emeritus
Lifeway Christian Stores
2017

Table of Contents

Preface

My father was a Baptist pastor all my childhood years, and I learned much about the offices of pastor and deacon watching him shepherd and lead with servant-hearted diligence. The deacons I came to know growing up were not perfect, but God worked through them to leave a positive impression on me. That influence continues to shape me today and has played a foundational role in the development of *A Deacon On Purpose*.

I began as a music minister ("song leader," as they called me) at a normative-sized church in South Louisiana when I was seventeen years old, the summer before my senior year of high school. The deacons there encouraged my role at the church. They were influential in the early years of my marriage and instrumental in my spiritual growth in life and ministry. I thank God they took a chance on a skinny, clueless, high school boy who had not the slightest idea what God had in store for his future. Twenty-five years later, I still reflect with amazement on how God used those men to sustain and strengthen me.

In May 2017, after eighteen years serving local churches in Texas and Louisiana as a pastor, music minister, discipleship leader, and Christian counselor, God called me to service in the larger family of Baptist cooperation as the Director of Pastor|Church Relations (later, Associate Executive Director) for the Southern Baptists of Texas Convention. Over the course of those eighteen years in local church ministry, I had the honor of meeting, being discipled by, and working closely with hundreds of faithful deacons. Even in the years that followed, while working with the Convention through the course of five interim pastorates in six years, deacons in each church were invaluable to the organizational stability and spiritual vitality of the churches I shepherded through transition.

Some of them have taken their heavenward flight, and I await, with joyful anticipation, the day of our reunion in glory. Others I have known through the years and am privileged to still call on as friends for wisdom and encouragement. Faithful, godly, Spirit-led deacons have been invaluable to my spiritual journey from my earliest memories to this very day. Some of their stories are included in this book. However, no record but heaven's could contain the inexhaustible treasures of positive influence these faithful servants of Christ's churches have had in my life.

Upon assuming my role in pastoral care and leadership at the Convention in Texas, I searched for resources to assist us in training deacons across the state. At that time, the most recent deacon training books I might have considered were over a decade old. Robert Naylor, president of Southwestern Baptist Theological Seminary, published *The Baptist Deacon* in 1955 and Howard B. Foshee of the Baptist Sunday School Board followed with *Now that You're a Deacon* in 1975. Both were valuable in their time. In 2008, Lifeway Christian Resources published *The Deacon I Want to Be*, complete with workbooks, worsksheets, and videos. The resource was helpful and insightful in its time, but a little too detailed and complex for some deacons in normative sized churches. Where was the contemporary, practical, easily readable deacon training resource for the third decade of the twenty-first century? The Holy Spirit impressed upon me that this needed resource was in my heart and in my head. It just needed to be worked out and written down.

I completed the first draft of *A Deacon On Purpose* in the summer of 2017. Then, after several rounds of editing by my friend and coworker Gary Ledbetter, it was graphically formatted and printed by the Southern Baptists of Texas Convention. It was an immediate success. For six years I travelled across Texas and many other states holding church and associational deacon trainings. Two years in, I trained my state convention staff to lead deacon trainings themselves so that the work could be multiplied. And it was, exponentially. We could not keep enough copies of the book on hand to satisfy the growing demand. The resource was translated into other languages and made available in a free, online PDF form. I began receiving emails literally from church leaders all over the world offering thanksgiving for *A Deacon On Purpose* as they were using it to train their deacons. It is both humbling and rewarding to know that the influence of hundreds of deacons all over Texas and Louisiana, whom God placed in my life over many years, has laid the foundation for a resource like this. Their love for Christ and devotion to his church continues to strengthen deacon bodies all over the world. Their legacy lives in the proliferation of their stories and exemplary obedience to Christ, through *A Deacon On Purpose*.

Since 2017, several other helpful resources for deacon training have come on the market. I met Andy Spencer, a faithful deacon in a Texas church, in 2018 and learned that he and his pastor Michael Lewis had recently co-authored a book entitled, *Lift Your Pastor: Becoming a Pastor's Advocate*. In it they build on their unique friendship through the years to offer ten practical ways a deacon can serve the church by supporting his pastor. *On Being A Deacon* by Mark Hallock and several of his deacons was published in 2019. It's an excellent, practical tool in the hands of any deacon or deacon body. In 2021, 9Marks (with Crossway Publishing) published Matt Smethurst's *Deacons* which has done wonders for biblically repositioning deacons in Baptist churches, especially among the reformed tradition. In 2023, executive director Todd Gray with several Kentucky Baptists authored an intensely practical tool for deacons under the title *The Deacon Ministry Handbook*. Also, I would be negligent if I did not include Lifeway's *Deacon Magazine* in this brief survey of helpful, contemporary resources. *Deacon Magazine*, edited by my friend and Hawaii-Pacific Baptist Convention executive director Craig Webb, has provided contemporary and contextual encouragement to deacons for more than fifty years. I regularly recommend all of these resources to deacons and deacon bodies who desire to be sharpened and strengthened in their service to Christ's churches.

In the spring of 2023, God called me to service among South Carolina Baptists. Upon arrival, I quickly realized that *A Deacon On Purpose*, so graciously promoted and distributed by the Southern Baptists of Texas Convention for six years, needed to be updated and revised for its next season of usefulness to Christ's churches. My friend Jeff Robinson, editor and president for *The Baptist Courier*, agreed to carry the second edition through their newly branded ministry publishing arm, and it has been a joy to work with him and his staff through the process.

So, with the proliferation of new deacon training resources since 2017, why is a second edition of *A Deacon On Purpose* necessary? Allow me to offer several reasons. First, while the first edition was intensely practical and proved broadly helpful, it was limited by my knowledge and experience at the time. By God's grace, I have learned so much more over these last seven years as I have brushed shoulders with more and more people who hold this biblical office. Many of the updates in this second edition reflect my own sharpened understanding. I'm grateful for the influence of even more deacons who are now forever part of my story—and I, theirs.

Secondly, *A Deacon On Purpose* suggests a unique, concise, easily understood paradigm for deacon ministry. It lives at the 30,000 ft. level and only dives lower momentarily to make practical suggestions that may or may not be beneficial in your deacon body. Some of the other new resources major on the minors, and I am grateful for their attention to detail and concentrated practicality. But the four purposes herein are clear and simple, easily translatable into the deacon body of any church, regardless of church size or culture. The discussion questions and reflection points at the end of each chapter are aimed at cultivating an environment conducive to self-assessed, self-driven, contextualized application.

Thirdly, the availability of the printed resource has not been able to keep up with demand. The Southern Baptists of Texas Convention has worked hard at keeping the books in stock, but the Convention is not a publishing agency. This new arrangement with the South Carolina *Baptist Courier's* publishing arm ensures that supply will keep up with demand in the present and for the future. This second edition is available through popular online webstores and other avenues through which books are more typically acquired. The resource is now more readily and consistently available to individual deacons, church leaders, associational and convention leaders, and anyone else who may find value in its pages.

Finally, for centuries evangelical literature was deprived of biblically centered, practically helpful deacon training resources. As the twenty-first century continues to unfold, and as the rapidity of technological and social change continues to surge, we need more—not less—resources aimed at encouraging and training candidates for and holders of this important biblical office. In 2017, I felt as if I were all alone with *A Deacon On Purpose*. Today, by God's grace, I feel like *A Deacon On Purpose* is one tool in a drawer of many that, together, offer a more comprehensive approach to deaconing well.

As you read through the following pages, my encouragement is to do so slowly and prayerfully and to refer to it often as you serve in the office of deacon. I never intend to write books for hurried consumption. I expect that the more you consult these pages in the coming months and years, the more God will reveal spiritual, ideological, and practical insight for the passing seasons. You are not a deacon on accident. So, be a deacon on purpose. My only victory in this work would be to know that, in some small way, the following pages give biblical and practical shape to your journey as a deacon in Christ's church. May it be so.

"Let the favor of the Lord our God be on us; establish for us the
work of our hands—establish the work of our hands."

(Psalm 90:17)

Chapter 1

Introduction

Y ou are not a mistake. Your call to be a deacon is not a mistake. Your whole life, God has been molding you and shaping you. He has for his grand design the image of his Son Jesus Christ (2 Corinthians 3:18). Admittedly, we are all extremely far from that finished product right now. But we are progressing toward it. You were lost and dead in sin, but God redeemed you through repentance and faith in Jesus. He deposited his Holy Spirit within you and set your feet on the path of wisdom, a journey that will one day end in your own glory when you step out of this sin-scarred world and into your eternal heavenly home. But God is still molding and shaping you even now. Like a potter modeling his clay, he is making you into the man or woman he has called and newly created you to be.

And look at you now. Would you have thought—ten years ago, twenty years ago—that God would have called you to be a deacon in his church? A servant-leader in his created and chosen vehicle for worldwide gospel propagation? "Unworthy" is the only word that comes to my mind when I think about God's call on my life. But praise God, he has made me worthy through his son Jesus. And it is now my goal to "serve well" for God's glory and for the strengthening of my own faith (1 Timothy 3:13).

Your local church family has seen within you the qualities they desire in a deacon. They have called you to serve them. To love them. To lead them. God has ordained. You have surrendered. The church has appointed. Yours is a high calling, one that thrusts you underneath the weight of other congregants' first-world problems, lifting them up and encouraging them in their walk of faith. God has called. The church has approved. You have answered.

So, you're a deacon. Now what?

Not too long ago, I sat in a deacon ordination ceremony at a church where I had been blessed to accomplish some meaningful ministry. Although Sunday morning gatherings there draw thousands, the deacon ordination service was held in a small chapel where a couple dozen church members gathered for the occasion. Most of them were either existing deacons or family members of the two being presented for ordination. I wondered about the general lack of interest in a ceremony like this. As far as I know, the church places a high value on its deacons and their service. But attendance at the ordination ceremony that Sunday evening fell remarkably short of that morning's worship service attendance. Many factors were in play, I'm sure. People are busy. The Sunday evening block in this church's programming is generally reserved for family time and rest. No children's activities were scheduled. The list goes on. But I trust the Lord brought those to this ceremony who he wanted to be there.

The service was moving and meaningful. The pastor brought a solid biblical charge from Acts 6:1–7. The deacons gathered around the candidates and their young families, laid hands on them, and prayed. The prayers were full of sincerity and expectation. The simultaneous audible petitions of many seasoned saints filled the room. I could almost smell the sweet aroma of intercession as it rose heavenward. Men and women prayed for the candidates' families. They prayed for renewed and increasing spiritual fervor in those the congregation had newly set apart for this office. Then they prayed for each candidate's commitment to the church's mission and vision, the community's lost and wandering souls, the pastor's bold but servant-hearted leadership, and the church members' spiritual zeal to engage in the Great Commission. The deacon chair offered a final prayer on behalf of them all, and the ceremony concluded with a revivifying spiritual lift. Sitting on the back pew, hearing the saints pray with hope and power, I wished the whole church body would have experienced the solemn intensity of that expectant moment.

I shook the candidates' hands on their way out the door and thanked them for their willingness to serve Christ's bride in this official role. I saw something strange on their faces, though. It was almost like the whole journey culminated here, at the ordination service. Behind their glazed pupils rested a strange mix of relief and disquiet. No doubt, the church's yearlong testing and shadowing phase was taxing. Preparation for the ordination council's questions was intense. Faith and family had been tested through the lengthy process. Perhaps this ceremony felt more like an arrival point for them than a commencement. Deep in the recesses of their orbital cavities I sensed a hungry, contingent curiosity. From each of them, I could almost hear the silent words that fogged their gazes but dared not escape their lips: I'm a deacon. Now what?

That thought passes through my mind every time I take part in a deacon ordination service. Most churches have outlined specific, biblical qualifications for prospective deacons. Most have a well-defined process for their selection. Most have general guidelines for deacon activity after they are installed. But when it comes to the daily, weekly, and monthly rhythms of serving as a deacon, many churches do not have an intentional plan for training new deacons or for sharpening existing deacons as the years pass. This study, *A Deacon On Purpose*, is designed to meet that need. Perhaps you will use this as a training tool for potential or newly selected deacons. Or perhaps you will use it as a refresher course for deacons who have served for decades. In any case, *A Deacon on Purpose* will call the deacon body back to a biblical framework for service in the church.

There are many excellent structural approaches to organizing the functions of the deacon body. Different structures and strategies will fit different churches well, according to their specific needs and their deacons' specific gifts. Your church may employ a deacon family ministry model, a ministry team leadership model, a shepherding group model, or any number of other paradigms. This study is not about structures and strategies. Rather, the goal herein is overall purpose. From the Bible, I see four general biblical purposes to deacon ministry in the church. Whatever strategy or structure your deacon body utilizes, it must in some way facilitate these four biblical purposes. Each of the four purposes is explained, illustrated, and practically applied in the subsequent chapters. At the end of each chapter, you will find questions for group reflection and discussion that will hopefully cultivate an environment that facilitates thoughtful, creative contextualization.

I encourage you to use *A Deacon on Purpose* as a guide to equip your deacons toward their four biblical purposes in the church. Repeat this training systematically when new deacons begin their service. Use it to challenge the status quo and draw existing deacons back to their biblical purpose. As I have led deacon trainings on this material all over the United States the past seven years, I have told deacon bodies that they should walk away with a hundred ideas but decide on only one or two to implement over the next six to twelve months. The goal of trainings like this is not to perfect your deacon body overnight. Rather, the goal is to keep you all moving forward, together. Pick one thing and work on it. Six to twelve months later, pick something else.

Be intentional about this. The church functions well when it is led well and served well. It is my prayer that this will be a tool in your church's hands toward servant-hearted leadership within your deacon body and that the gospel of Jesus Christ will advance because of it.

Our case study for the four biblical purposes of deacon ministry is Acts 6:1–7. Although these seven men may not have been formally called "deacons," this important passage sets the stage for formal deacon ministry in the local New Testament Church. Recently, Matt

Smethurst has called this passage a "blueprint" for the deaconate: "These [seven] men are forerunners who essentially preview the formal role that deacons will soon hold in local churches."[1] I couldn't agree more. Verses 2–3 set forth the responsibility of these chosen men as *diakonein trapezais*, to "serve tables." To be a deacon is to serve and to model servant leadership. You will read and reflect on Acts 6:1–7 often as you work through *A Deacon On Purpose*. But let's begin with the end. Verse 7 reveals what happened among the church as a direct result of these seven men serving well:

> "So the word of God spread, the disciples in Jerusalem increased greatly in number, and a large group of priests became obedient to the faith." (Acts 6:7)

That's the whole point. Isn't this what you want to see in your church, also? "The word of God spread." The written word of God, by the power of the Holy Spirit, frees people from shame, gives them life, secures lasting hope, illuminates every path ahead, and satisfies the longing heart (Psalm 119:6, 40, 81, 105, 162). Imagine if these Psalm 119 promises became realized in your community. Imagine if your neighbors and friends came to know God and to live in the freedom of his righteous love through the effective spreading of his written word.

"The disciples … increased greatly in number." More and more people repented and believed the gospel. Church growth is not a goal in itself, but the book of Acts does not shy away from celebrating exponential increases in the number of people who have been saved, baptized, and assimilated into the body-life of the church (Acts 2:41, 47; 5:14; 6:1, 7; etc.). We all want to see the same happen in our church families, don't we?

"And a large group of priests became obedient to the faith." Even the most biblically knowledgeable among them grew deeper in knowledge of and obedience to the ways of God. I'm certain there are members of your church who have walked with God for a long time. Don't you long to see them grow even deeper in their faith and faithfulness to Christ? I'm not saying this is a secret formula for church growth. But at a minimum, we have to acknowledge that, at least in the first-century Jerusalem church, verse 7 happened on the heels of verses 1–6. When deacons serve the church well, on purpose, the gospel is advanced, the Great Commission is fulfilled, and people grow deeper into their faith in Jesus. Another has suggested that without the deaconing ministry of Acts 6:1–6, "the gospel would not have spread" as it did: "The work of a deacon, then, is freighted with significance. Its effects will reverberate into eternity."[2]

The significance of a biblical deacon ministry cannot be overstated. Yours is a vital calling. Serve well and you will advance the cause of Christ; serve halfheartedly and you will hinder it. Your time is too short and your mission too important to be a deacon on accident. So, be a deacon on purpose.

Questions for Group Reflection/Discussion

1. Reflect on (share) your story. How did you come to faith in Christ? How did you know he was calling you to be a deacon? What is God doing in your life today as he continues to shape and mold you into the image of Christ?

2. Read Acts 6:1–7. What are some initial observations you can draw from the text, and how do/should those observations inform the role/office of the deacon in a local church?

3. Take some time to work through your church's structure for accomplishing the functions of the deacon body. Do not burden yourself just yet with what *should* be. Rather, just work to agree on what is. What do deacons at your church do? How are they selected? What standards of character and/or accountability exist?

"In those days, as the disciples were increasing in number, there arose a complaint by the Hellenistic Jews against the Hebraic Jews that their widows were being overlooked in the daily distribution. The Twelve summoned the whole company of the disciples and said, 'It would not be right for us to give up preaching the word of God to wait on tables. Brothers and sisters, select from among you seven men of good reputation, full of the Spirit and wisdom, whom we can appoint to this duty. But we will devote ourselves to prayer and to the ministry of the word.' This proposal pleased the whole company. So they chose Stephen, a man full of faith and the Holy Spirit, and Philip, Prochorus, Nicanor, Timon, Parmenas, and Nicolaus, a convert from Antioch. They had them stand before the apostles, who prayed and laid their hands on them. So the word of God spread, the disciples in Jerusalem increased greatly in number, and a large group of priests became obedient to the faith."

(Acts 6:1–7)

Chapter 2

Lead By Example

Southern Baptists, whom I serve, confess two "offices" in the local New Testament church: pastor and deacon.[3] In many ways, you could call the pastor the lead leader. Under the authority of Jesus Christ and the guidance of the Holy Spirit, he sets the overall direction and vision of the church. He is not the only leader in the church. That's ridiculous. The church is full of leaders. As Peter Drucker famously intimated in the 1990s, "The only definition of a leader is someone who has followers."[4] Whether you like it or not, eighth-grade girls are leading fifth-grade girls, senior boys are leading freshman boys, and senior adults are leading younger adults. They are leaders because others are following. The question is not "will they lead?" but "who are they leading, and where?" Thoughtful pastors don't own all leadership in the church. Rather, they lead leaders in the church.

Similarly, deacons are the lead servants. I have a hard time imagining that when the Acts 6 deacons were chosen, the rest of the congregation sighed in relief and thought, "Thank goodness, we do not have to serve people ever again." The deacons were not chosen as the *only* servants of the church. They were chosen as the *lead* servants of the church. They set the tone, the direction, and the culture of servant leadership. Faithful deacons are God's gift to the church "to both serve the membership and set the example for their faith and practice."[5]

In our biblical case study (Acts 6:1–7), the verb used in verse 2 to describe the expected duty of the selected men is *diakoneo*. It is the same word from which we have derived our English word "deacon." The word for "deacon" literally means, in both form and function, *servant*.

Deacon Body, Not Deacon Board

Local churches were undoubtedly influenced by the proliferation of business practices and the organizational revolution brought about in the early-to-mid twentieth century. In some ways, this influence was good and healthy. Not until the early twentieth century had churches considered budgeting for annual ministry needs. The organizational practices born out of a wartime, centralized government influenced my own denomination's missions funding strategy. Increasing global awareness spring-boarded opportunities for international missions.

But not all influence was good and healthy. This same business-minded approach to church life became fertile soil for a growing trend in local churches in which deacons would run the business affairs of the church while the pastor(s) would work the ministry of the church. Well-meaning as this separation was, it created the opportunity for power-play dynamics between the two New Testament offices. Instead of working together in ministry and church administration, pastors and deacons were often at odds with each other. Instead of seeing the deacons and pastors as coworkers in local church ministry, some pastors began to feel increasing pressure from their deacons to perform and meet expectations (even if those expectations were sometimes uncommunicated). Instead of focusing their time and energy on ministering to ("serving") the congregation, many deacon bodies became nothing more than administrative boards within a church's decision-making structure. When business efficiency and church power-play dynamics courted, the so-called deacon board was born.

But a deacon body is not a board. In 1975, Howard B. Foshee of the Baptist Sunday School Board addressed the issue forthrightly:

"The unfortunate term 'board of deacons' ... is foreign to the way Baptists should work together under the leadership of the Holy Spirit."[6] Biblically, deacons do not gather in secret meetings to influence church polity and practice. They do not meet regularly to make decisions that others should follow. They do not guard the finances, direct the ministry, or serve as a cog in a wheel of checks and balances within a congregation. Deacons love with the heart of Christ, serve with the hands of Christ, think with the mind of Christ, speak with the voice of Christ, and go with the feet of Christ. They are active agents of Christ's selfless ministry within and through his local churches. Together, they are not an institution, but an organism. Not a board, but a body.

Model Servants

Deacons are the lead servants of Christ's churches. However, service in the church has never been restricted to those who hold the title of deacon. The Bible instructs all members of the Body of Christ to serve one another. Consider Peter's instructions in 1 Peter 4:10: "Just as each one has received a gift, use it to serve others, as good stewards of the varied grace of God," (see also 2 Corinthians 8:19, 2 Timothy 1:18, Philemon 1:13, and Hebrews 6:10). It is the calling of every Christian to serve others in the church body with the giftedness God has afforded him or her.

But the deacon has been called beyond this general instruction into an official position of service within the church. All Christians are called to perform the actions of sacrificial service. But the deacon is called to a biblical office, to lead by example in this Christian standard of excellence. Deacons are expected to be servant-leaders, models of what it means to be a good steward of the "varied grace of God."

When the members of your church look at you, deacon, they should see the model servant. They should see someone leading not by extortion or exasperation, but by example. Thus, the first biblical purpose of the deacon is to be an exemplary leader.

My memory of him is so vivid. To this day, almost forty years later, I could describe to you the curvature of his face, the wrinkles on the backs of his hands, the way his eyes lit up when he talked about the church. His name was Bro. Kendall. He was a faithful deacon in the church my dad pastored. I cannot remember many times I was at church when he was not there. He was always present. Always working. Always supportive. Always encouraging. Always faithful.

Bro. Kendall took a rotation on the bus route, and when it was not his turn to drive, he always had boxes of donuts waiting for us kids when we arrived. He mowed grass, painted walls, fixed coffee, and taught Sunday School. He helped with RA's and came every day of Vacation Bible School to offer his assistance wherever needed. I remember shaking his warm, firm hands and receiving that infectious smile of his approval—not approval of what I had done, just approval of who I was. To him, I wasn't the pastor's son or some rowdy bus kid who needed to be reined in. I was just Tony. I admit that, at the time, I did not know how much that meant to me.

Bro. Kendall prayed the most eloquent prayers. His feet floated across the floor when he served the Lord's Supper, and his eyes smiled at every person who received it from his hand. He was a man of integrity. And character. And grace. One Sunday morning during my dad's sermon, Bro. Kendall drew his last breath and quietly slipped away into Heaven with Jesus. I admit, I was a bit freaked out about it when I was a kid (as were many more in church that morning). But knowing what I know now about Bro. Kendall's love for God and for his church, there is no more fitting way for him to have slipped into eternity. I wanted to be like him. I still do.

Leading by Influence

By nature of the office, deacons have both positional and relational influence in the church. Positional influence is the least effective of the two, but it is still inherent to the office. Positional influence happens when someone leverages a title or formal authority to enforce a decision or effect change. Can you imagine pulling out your deacon card and slapping it down on the table in front of that gossiping widow? "Listen, you're going to stop spreading these rumors because I'm a deacon and I said so." Or pointing to your deacon nametag when that unruly young neighborhood boy can't seem to keep still in his seat? "I'm a deacon, and you're going to sit still." Let me know how that works out for you.

Positional influence is real to the diaconate, however. Rare occasions will arise when leveraging the positional influence of the office is necessary in fulfilling the other purposes of your ministry. But allow me to caution you here. These instances are so rare and so serious that you should not leverage positional influence alone as a deacon. Rather, if positional influence is to be leveraged from the deacon office, it should be leveraged as a whole deacon body with one voice, never as one individual deacon. For example, some pastors may lean upon their deacon body in issues of church discipline. Other pastors may see benefit in having a deacon body lead the charge in a church-wide ministry project or vision shift. Whatever the occasion, remember that positional influence is often not necessary and usually not as effective as you might think.

However, relational influence is a great motivator toward positive congregational movement. And because you are a deacon, you can build relationships with the people in your church (at a minimum, the ones under your direct care or ministry assignment), and organically influence them through your relationship and by your personal example. As I have written elsewhere, "Christianity is an up-close faith."[7] The invitation to leadership in the Christian community is first and foremost an invitation to come be with us— to come be us. "You multiply your ministry—you outlive your life— when you enter someone else's space in humility, and by humility, allow that someone into your space too."[8]

That's the sweet spot of relational influence. It's right there, in the middle space of intentional togetherness between a deacon and a church member. When members of the church engage in the mission because they feel like they should or like they must, their buy-in is usually weak and short-lived. But if they engage because they want to and because they respect and love others around them on the same journey, they're in for life. Deacons should be loving and respectful around other church members, building healthy relationships and positively influencing fellow Christians toward the mission of the church. They should live in the middle space of intentional togetherness within the church they are called to serve. Positional influencers stand a head above. Relational influencers stand shoulder-to-shoulder. The latter makes for a more reciprocally fulfilling partnership along the journey of faith.

Want to know a secret? You are always influencing people. Especially as someone with a "title" in the church, you don't get away from exerting influence. You don't get to take off your deacon hat at the ball game, in the grocery store, or behind that phone screen. Wherever you are and whoever you are with, you are leveraging influence. By your action or inaction, your speech or silence, your involvement or absence, you are always influencing people. When you accepted the call to the diaconate, you gave up your right to ask, "Do I want to influence people today?" The question is not "Will I influence?" Only, "Who?" and "How?" In his 1975 *Now That You're A Deacon*, Howard B. Foshee articulated the principle compellingly: "Once a person is elected a deacon, he no longer has a choice as to whether he will set an example. The only decision concerns the kind of example he will be."[9]

Here are four areas of church life in which deacons must lead by personal example.

Attendance

Ask any pastor you know. His idea of the model church member always includes, on the most basic level, being present in church gatherings. And you, deacon, are leading by example. Members need to be present in order to be a part of the body-life of the church. Perhaps that's what frustrated the writer of Hebrews as he explained the importance of corporate worship, encouragement, and account-ability (Hebrews 10:24–25). When someone is regularly present, his or her absence is felt. When regularly absent, his or her presence is awkward. When believers are disconnected from the church body for a season, they fall away easily, and it is often difficult to jump back into a moving stream from which you have been removed for a while.

Your church has a regular schedule of activities for a reason. Obviously, it is impossible for every single person to make every single worship service or church gathering. But absence should be the exception, not the rule. Some church members work shifts that disallow them to be present every Sunday. Others work overseas 6 months out of the year. Of course, serious illnesses or injuries will keep almost every Christian from church at some point in his or her life. As a general rule, when church members are in town and healthy, they should gather with their church families. Announcements, vision state-ments, biblical doctrines, and church-specific decisions are communi-cated weekly in scheduled gatherings. When a church member is often physically absent from the body-life, he or she is at risk of being spiri-tually and relationally absent from the body-life as well.

But you know that. You are spiritually mature and maturing. You know all too well that there are members of your congregation who constantly vacillate between being committed and being unengaged. It is most likely part of your weekly or monthly assignment to reach out and connect with these wandering sheep in attempts to gently bring them back into the fold. You know that God has big plans for them in his church. You know that he has gifted them uniquely through the work of the Holy Spirit, and that your church desperately needs them to use that giftedness for its edification and for God's glory. You know these things.

So, what are you communicating to your church members by your own attendance habits? How does your regular presence, or regular absence, influence the vacillators in your church body? Every week there are a million things vying for their time and devotion: children's sports leagues, major professional ballgames, dirty houses, hunting season, warm beds after long sleepless nights, beautiful sunshine, pouring rain. The excuses are legion. Every week, the people you lead battle the temptation to be somewhere else, rather than in the church gathering.

Do they see in you a model of faithful attendance? You contend with all the same potential distractions they do. But are you committed to the body-life, like they should be committed to the body-life? Your regular attendance, or regular absence, leads people by way of positional and relational influence. You are leading by example. As a general rule, whatever freedoms you exercise in moderation they will adopt in excess. I promise you this: if there are deacons in your deacon body who do not commit to the body-life of the church, you will begin to observe a spiraling, unmanageable sense of detachment among the people in your pews.

This point should be wholly unnecessary. I wish it had no need of being said. However, for almost a decade I have consulted with too many deacon bodies (usually, "boards") that are populated by office holders who do not attend church. They come to Sunday School but leave before the worship service. Or they stopped attending altogether because they don't like the music, the sanctuary remodel, or the pastor's business casual attire. It's ridiculous. Can you imagine if every church member boycotted the church gatherings because of some personal vendetta or personal preference? Deacons, you are leading by example, and you need to be more committed (and more spiritually mature) than this. Honestly, your commitment to regularly scheduled church activities is just a beginning. This is a minimum. It is literally the lowest level of commitment you can possibly have as a servant leader in your church. Attend faithfully. It's not complicated. Now let's dive into the deeper waters of leadership by example.

Ministry Involvement

The same pastor who expects the model church member to attend services also expects the model church member to be involved. Church members should not just sit and soak, they should actively produce something, according to their spiritual giftedness, as an integral part of the ministry model of the church. Do you serve on any ministry teams? Are you active in the mission projects of your church? Do people in your church regularly see you serving as a faithful volunteer? If you don't, they won't. Leading the church from the deacon chair is a matter of modeling good church membership. Those things your pastor and staff want your church members to be doing, you should be consistently modeling.

It takes every member for the church to be effective in its mission. Consider Paul's words to the church in Ephesus: "From him [(Christ)] the whole body, fitted and knit together by every supporting ligament, promotes the growth of the body for building up itself in love by the proper working of each individual part," (Ephesians 4:16). When the parts of the body (members of the church) do not serve the mission of the church by using the giftedness God has afforded them, the church body is not being built up. It becomes stagnant at best, dying at worst. But why would church members give their precious time and energy to be an active part of something when church leaders don't?

Imagine the ministry departments of your church as lanes on a running track. You have a children's ministry lane, a music ministry lane, a senior adult ministry lane, a Sunday School ministry lane, an A/V ministry lane, etc. My encouragement to you, as a servant leader, is to pick a lane and run in it, but do not own the lane. Healthy, mature Christians disciple, mentor, and then release other Christians to meaningful ministry. They do not lock down ministry opportunities and exclude multiplicative service.

For example, let's say Deacon Benny has run the sound board for forty years. Pastor John decides one Sunday morning to use him as a living example of what it looks like to be devoted and dedicated to ministry in the church. He pulls Deacon Benny on stage and says, "This is what faithful, servant-hearted ministry looks like." The congregation claps and Deacon Benny returns to his post. What did Pastor John just do? He celebrated that in forty years one of his deacons has never taught another person to run the sound board. What happens when Deacon Benny dies? And how many gifted believers have passed through the church in forty years who could have been discipled, mentored, trained, and released into A/V ministry either in this church or another?

A better celebration would have been something like, "In forty years Deacon Benny has trained twenty-three men and women on the sound board, several of which take a weekly rotation here and others are involved in churches all over the region. Because Deacon Benny saw the A/V ministry as a pathway for reproduction, his influence is felt among the larger Body of Christ right now and will be felt for generations to come here at our local church." Now that's the way to leverage servant oriented relational influence. Who will train the next generation of ushers, musicians, teachers, preachers, evangelists, and missionaries if not deacons in your church?

To be a faithful deacon is to "be about the business of reproducing" yourself in the lives of the next generation. As one author wrote, "If your deacon body is not intentional about incubating, investing in, mentoring, and entrusting the work to the next generation of servant leaders, every kingdom advance you have worked so hard to gain will die a slow and painful death."[10] Another has written, "As a deacon you are an exemplar leader. In addition to finding and using your gifts for God, be a part of stirring up the gifts of others."[11]

Deacon, you do not need to be involved in every ministry area. But you do need to find a lane and run in it. And you need to find or invent ways to reproduce yourself inside those lanes. You can encourage church members to get on track and run on mission together until you are blue in the face. But if you don't, they won't.

Tithing & Giving

The pastor expects a model church member to come to church gatherings and to be involved in church ministry. Don't you think he also expects the model church member to be financially invested in the work? Your pastor may or may not see the tithe as a biblical instruction for today. But I would bet my bottom Baptist dollar that he has some kind of vision, built on biblical instruction, for how he expects church members to steward their financial resources sacrificially and cheerfully. Why would church members give sacrificially and cheerfully to God's kingdom work in and through their local church if their leaders do not?

As a deacon, you are to model good stewardship of the financial resources God has entrusted to you. Your pastor appreciates your time and service, but let's get real—financial resources are needed to run electricity, fund ministry areas, plan activities, pay salaries, promote visions, and operate with excellence. Too many deacons are merely *bought in* to God's kingdom work in and through their local church. What the church needs from you is not to be bought in, but to be *sold out*.

I am not advocating any kind of public disclosure of your giving (although I have known churches to do so). Your giving is between you, God, and your pastor. I personally believe there should be no bragging, publication, or announcement of the deacon's giving practices. However, when tested against your pastor's expectations for church members, you, deacon, should have been exceeding the mark. Church members do not select deacons like nonprofits select board members. You are not in this seat because of your potential to financially contribute to the church's mission and vision substantially. You are not here because you are a brilliant business owner, a prominent community member, a proven fundraiser, or a wealthy private philanthropist. You are here because you are faithful to Christ and to his church, called by God and affirmed by the membership as someone who can lead by example in an official place of sacrificial servitude.

God owns the cattle on a thousand hills (Ps 50:10). The earth is the Lord's and everything in it (Ps 24:1–2). He already owns everything you have and everything your church members have. God is not pacing the floors of Heaven wishing he had more money in your church's bank account. But he is moving in the hearts of his people to trust him more and more with that which he has entrusted to their stewardship. All the resources of heaven flow through the hands of Christ's people (Eph 1:3). The only question is to what extent Christ's people are willing to live with open hands. You're church's problem is not financial shortfall, and its solution is not financial gain. The problem is disobedient hearts, and the solution is open hands. And deacon, you are leading by example.

One of the greatest honors of being a Christ follower is to allow the riches of heaven to flow through the channels of obedience liberally and unobstructed. The ability to give to God's kingdom work through your local church is a great blessing. This ability is, in itself, a gift from God. He is the One who "provides seed for the sower and bread for food," and it is he who "will also provide and multiply your seed and increase the harvest of your righteousness" (2 Corinthians 9:10). It is amazing how generous giving through your local church produces a singular devotion to God's kingdom work. It is also amazing how, no matter where you keep it, your pocketbook is always in close proximity to your heart. Deacon, give freely. Give lavishly. Give cheerfully. And in so doing, lead by example.

Attitude (On and Off the Court)

Years ago, I watched an interview with a college basketball coach who was talking about the kinds of players he recruited. He explained that there are many talented kids in the game these days and deciding who to recruit is always difficult. For that reason, one of the very first things this coach evaluates is not the player's skill, but his attitude. The coach already knows the kid's got game;

otherwise, he would not have made the trip. Instead, he watches how the player acts toward officials, teammates, and the opposing team. But get this. The recruiting coach said he is not just watching the player while he is in the game. He's watching him while he's on the bench as well! He wants to see a potential recruit be the first one to join the huddle. He wants to see him hanging on every word as the coach corrects and instructs. He wants to see him celebrating teammates' good efforts, respecting coaching decisions, and itching to get back in the game when the coach says it's time.

If the player has a bad attitude either on or off the court, this college coach says, "I don't want him on my team." If he can't run the court with a good attitude, and if he can't sit the bench with a good attitude, the player will be a disease on the team, not an asset. He may be incredibly talented. He may have a natural giftedness in the game. But players' attitudes are contagious, and this coach doesn't want a negative attitude affecting other players on his team.

Deacons need to have a positive, encouraging attitude both on and off the court. At a church I served many years ago, a deacon sat on the third row every Sunday with his arms crossed and a frown on his face. He refused to sing the songs, make eye contact with me as the pastor, or vote in favor of anything at business meetings. One day, at a business meeting, it became obvious that his attitude had affected several other members of the congregation. He had staged a coup. I sat down and another deacon took over as moderator, bringing a calm and gracious conclusion to the meeting. The next morning, the deacon body called in their friend and fellow deacon to hold him accountable. "You're miserable here," I said out loud in that meeting. He was. The next week I caught him privately and told him I'd be glad to help him find a new church home in the area where he felt like he and his family could thrive and recapture the joy of their service to Christ and his church. He obliged. The last decade of his life, he and his family were more joyful, and our church was more successful in Christ's mission. I'll see him in heaven one day, and we will celebrate together endlessly and joyfully.

You may be amazed at how your attitude can be contagious. Keep a level head. Refuse to show negativity about your church's direction or its leadership, whether publicly or privately. The Apostle Paul instructed us toward this kind of Christian mindset: "Finally brothers and sisters, whatever is true, whatever is honorable, whatever is just, whatever is pure, whatever is lovely, whatever is commendable — if there is any moral excellence and if there is anything praiseworthy — dwell on these things," (Philippians 4:8). And if you cannot support the direction of the church, maybe you need to have a serious conversation with the pastor. Don't just sit and sour. Life is too short, and the kingdom of God is too big.

One of the most difficult things to get through as a church is a negative image within the body or the community. Every negative word feeds a negative image. Language creates culture. So, choose to focus on, speak about, and encourage others in what is praiseworthy. I bet if you really look at how God is working in your church, there is so much for which to be thankful. Promote those things. Talk about them. And watch how your positive attitude, on and off the court, will begin to change both your heart and the hearts of the church members you lead by example.

Conclusion

When my children were young, I would often look behind me and see them tracing my steps, awkwardly trying to mimic my stride or wear my facial expressions. It was cute and endearing. Now that they are young adults, I realize they are still watching me. Always. There is not a moment that goes by when I am not influencing them by action, word, or attitude. I pray daily that if they walk my walk, it will lead them to know God more fully and to love Him more deeply. I know that's a high expectation to place on my influence, but with great relational influence comes great spiritual responsibility.

Deacon, you lead by example. People are watching you. Always.

You are always influencing the people of your congregation, whether you want to or not, and your exemplary leadership will set the pace for their spiritual walk. What kind of pace are you modeling for them? If they follow in your steps, where will you lead them? If you ever wonder whether you are influencing positively or negatively through your leadership in the church, just look to the faces and listen to the voices of those who surround you. Their actions, words, and attitudes will tell the story of your leadership example. Good, bad, or ugly, over time you will see yourself in them.

Questions for Group Reflection/Discussion

1. Take a moment to celebrate some specific ways your church members are good at serving one another. Talk through how the example of the deacon body may have influenced this culture of biblical servitude.

2. In your own words, how is relational influence more powerful than positional influence?

3. Can you think of a deacon who influenced you positively at some point in the past? Say this person's name and give a short testimony to why.

4. When do you think it might be permissible to leverage positional influence as a deacon body?

5. Be honest with your fellow deacons: which of the four areas of leading by example do you need to work on the most right now?

Chapter 3

Serve the People

In the early 2000s, I was a young, developing minister of the gospel. I did not know it at the time, but the Lord was forming within me a philosophy of Christian leadership that would shape the way I served his churches for the rest of my life. To this point, I was not overly fond of reading. Knowing this, my pastor constantly pushed me. "Leaders are readers," he would say. Upon his recommendation, one of the first Christian leadership books I read was *Being Leaders* by Aubrey Malphurs (2003). That book bore immediate and lasting fruit in my ministry and kindled a flame for reading books on Christian theology, ministry, and leadership that nothing since has quenched.

As Malphurs reflects on Jesus's simple yet profound act of humility in John 13, he argues that love is the truest and most satisfying motivation for the work of servant leaders. The twelve disciples had accompanied him all over Galilee and performed powerful acts of ministry on their own. But despite all their practical and theological training in Jesus's school of real-life ministry, they were still a bunch of knuckleheads. In a harmony of the Gospel accounts, Jesus's foot washing object lesson came on the heels (pun intended) of an argument among the disciples regarding "who is the greatest," (Matthew 20:24–28, Luke 22:24–30). Jesus decided to resolve their debate not with an extended monologue or an authoritative correction, but with a self-deprecating act of service. He wrapped a towel around his waist; got down on his hands and knees; and scrubbed the dirty, stinky, calloused, mud-stained feet of his disciples, one of whom would soon betray him unto death. When Peter argued, "You will not wash me," Jesus replied, "You will have no part with me unless I wash you. ... The first will be last and the last will be first. ... The Son of Man came not to be served but to serve. ... I have given you an example, that you also should do just as I have done for you." Commenting on the cultural ignominy of this gesture, Malphurs writes, "We'll serve others humbly only to the degree that we love them. And the dirt on their feet will test our love for them."[12]

It is not a stretch for me to say this quote forever changed the way I see Christian ministry. To love someone Jesus's way requires humility, servitude, and sacrifice. Everywhere I go, Christ's people have dirty feet, and I am rarely more like Christ than when I assume a posture of humility to serve them selflessly. Deacons have the rare and special responsibility of serving Jesus's church. They wash the feet of Christ's Bride while he is preparing her for a wedding banquet yet to come. What love is this? What honor is yours? Love them, and you will serve them; serve them, and you will love them.

In Acts 6:2, the Apostles tell the people their greatest need is to focus on the work of preaching and leading instead of having to "wait on tables." Keep in mind, the apostles, serving as the pastor figures in this setting, began this widow ministry. They loved widows and wanted to serve them. The apostles did not see widows as a burden, and no evidence exists in the text that they wanted to pawn them off. They wanted to serve the widows, so they began a widow's ministry in the church. The apostles were providing daily staples for both the Hebrew widows and the Greek widows among them. But as the church grew, the task became too cumbersome and too time-consuming for the apostles themselves to manage it well. Some felt they were being unfairly left out, and maybe they were. So the idea for a New Testament deacon body was born in the context of a worthy yet humbling ministry: table-waiting on widows.

I cannot adequately emphasize the importance of this truth. The deacon ministry was born out of the need for service. These seven men were not chosen as a deacon board, making decisions for other people to follow. They were chosen to be men who were strong in the faith; full of the Spirit; wise in discretion; and willing to roll up their sleeves, put their feet to the floor, and serve the people of the church body. The second purpose of the New Testament deacon is good, old-fashioned, table-waiting service. You cannot be a deacon on purpose if you cannot or will not selflessly serve the people.

There are a number of practical ways that you can serve the membership as a deacon. Some of them can be systematized. Others must be spontaneous. However they are accomplished in your context, these things are non-negotiables for the deacon on purpose. Consider the following five areas of meaningful service.

Visitation

For five years, I pastored a normative size church in a very small, rural East Texas town. A modest hospital building was nestled in the slightly larger small town fifteen miles north of us, but it was not the place to go for much more than a few stitches or a twisted ankle. When church members checked into a hospital, they almost always travelled two hours north, one hour East, or forty-five minutes Southwest. Especially in the early months, with an aging congregation, I had a choice to make. I could either visit everyone in the hospital (and nursing homes, homebound, guests, etc.) or I could faithfully study and prepare for the three sermons I was to preach each week. I could not do both. Thankfully, only a few months into my tenure, Bro. Irv, a deacon, called at 8 a.m. one Monday morning. "Preacher, I'm on my way to Houston for business, and I left two hours early. Is there anyone I can stop and see for you on the way?" I felt immediate relief. One of our Sunday School teachers had checked into a hospital in that direction the night before and there was no way I could get down to see her. My deacon stepped into her room that morning with a smile on his face and said, "Mrs. Smith, Bro. Tony wanted to come this morning but just couldn't break away. He wants you to know he loves you and is praying for you. I'm here on his behalf. How are you doing?"

For the next five years, my deacon body became more and more intentional about sharing visitation responsibilities with me. They helped me visit nursing homes, first-time guests, couples in crisis, and much more. Over time, the members of our church and community knew that if they were in a season of crisis or concern, they could count on a deacon from our church to visit them. That ministry of presence opened the door for Great Commission advance in our little town more than any of us ever could have anticipated.

There is no way that your pastor and staff can make an appearance at every hospital, nursing home, home-bound need, milestone celebration, wedding, funeral, sports game, and widow's home and still be able to lead the church well. But deacons can be an extension of the pastor's ministry, the long arm of the pastor's sympathy, celebration, encouragement, and love. Often, deacons have scheduled visitation practices that are part of a systematic plan to ensure each member of the church is visited in his or her time of need. But most of the time, visitation needs pop up unexpectedly. Be an extension of your pastor's ministry by showing up at a hospital or cheering on your church's youth or children (by name) at a sporting event. If you get a chance, brag on your pastor while you're there. Give them his greeting and assure them of his love.

As a pastor, it made my heart smile to show up at a hospital and learn that one of my deacons had already been by to visit. One morning, I left my office the moment I heard that one of our widows, Mrs. Anna, had been hospitalized. When I walked in the door, she said, "Bro. Tony, it's so good to see you! Bro. Jody (a newly ordained deacon) just left. He heard I was in here and stopped by to see me on his lunch break. Isn't that sweet?!" Other times, I would get a call from a deacon who would say, "Johnny has had a rough week in the nursing home. There's no reason for you to go; I saw him yesterday and plan to go back tomorrow. I just wanted to keep you up to date." Those deacons were a gift from God not only to the church, but to me personally. They were an extension of my ministry. They served people by visiting them. And in doing so faithfully, they served me too.

Monthly Contacts

At least 51 percent of unchurched Americans say they would attend church if personally invited by a family member or close friend.[13] Isn't that amazing? Generally speaking, people in your community visit your church because someone they know and respect invited them. Not because they saw the church sign when they drove by, stumbled upon the website, or received that colorful flyer in the mail. Do you know why they stay? Because they get connected. Think about it. One of the warmest and most encouraging things guests and church members alike can say about your church is that it is a welcoming and friendly place where deep, lasting, and meaningful relationships are developed. Obviously, you and I know this only scratches the surface of the church's real value as a group of believers who are following Jesus together in likeminded fellowship. At the same time, however, it is undeniable that when people feel both socially and spiritually connected, they are more likely to stay, contribute, and grow.

As the church grows, it becomes more and more difficult for your church staff to keep up with everyone. If someone is engaged only when he or she walks through the church doors, meaningful relationships will be impossible to build. One Sunday morning, I noticed a church member whom I had not seen in a very long time. I approached her after the service and said, "Mrs. Johnson, I am so glad to see you today. I've been missing you." Her reply brought a smile to my face for reasons she probably will never know: "Thank you, Pastor. Bro. David (a deacon) has been keeping up with me.

He calls me about once a week. He and his wife came and picked me up this morning. It's so good to be able to be back with my church family." I was pleasantly surprised to know that one of my deacons and his wife had been keeping up with and ministering to this church member during an extended health crisis. I was disconnected from her personally. But because this deacon was intentional about his weekly contacts, she did not feel disconnected from me or from her church family.

In several of the churches I served as a pastor or interim, our deacons were given printed lists of families from our membership with whom they were responsible for staying connected throughout the course of a month. Some have called this a Family Ministry Plan. It's not complicated. The church's ministry assistant or clerk prints lists of the families in the church and divides by the number of deacons. Each deacon gets a list each month and makes sure to contact every family on the list with a text, phone call, home visit, hand-written card, etc.

SPECIAL RULES:

- Texting: (1) Do not group text. (2) Text only between 9 a.m. and 9 p.m. (3) If even the slightest chance exists that what you write might be inappropriate or perceived as such, don't text it. (4) Put transparency and accountability measures in place.
- Phone Call: (1) Do not be offended if people ignore your call; just leave a message and let it lie. (2) Generally, keep the conversation short. (3) Remove distractions around you so you can give the call your full attention.
- Home Visit: (1) Always call first. (2) Do not go alone; take your spouse, another deacon, or someone you are mentoring. (3) Do not ask to enter their home; if they invite you in, great, and if not, make your connection at the door with a smile.
- Handwritten Cards: (1) This will be the most meaningful form of connection to some. (2) Keep it short, just a few sentences.

(3) Offer a prayer or a Scripture quotation. (4) Sign your name legibly and include the name of your church.

+ Sporting Events: Sit next to the person or family at a local sporting event; there, you will likely have several hours to catch up while laughing and enjoying each other's company.

+ Mix It Up: Don't use the same communication method every month. Also, consider rotating lists so not every church/community member is always contacted by the same deacon.

Some churches depend upon their Sunday School or Small Group structure for monthly connections. That is good and healthy as well, so long as no one is getting left out. However you choose to organize it, every member (and regular attender) of your congregation needs to be contacted at least once every month. A church member will often need more frequent connections, depending on his or her season of life. Believe it or not, the biblical word "fellowship" is not Greek for "potluck" or "dinner on the grounds." Biblical fellowship is about a shared love, a shared purpose, and a shared life. It's a special sense of connected commonality among a group of born-again believers in Jesus Christ. That kind of fellowship must be cultivated if it is to grow.

At the end of Acts 2, when the church was experiencing conversion growth every day, one characteristic of their gathering was a special sense of connection. They were "devoted ... to the fellowship," "all the believers were together," and they "broke bread from house to house" (Acts 2:42–47). Our secular culture pulls us apart, but the culture of Christ's kingdom draws us together. The church must find a way to stay connected in a culture that is constantly dividing us. Church leaders must be intentional about this. Especially as we enter the middle of the twenty-first century, as the world feels smaller and smaller due to advancements in technology and travel, the people we are called to reach for Christ will have infinite opportunities to connect with affinity groups of their choosing. In those affinities, local or digital, they will find meaning, identity, and value. But the New Testament church has the monopoly on the truest sense of every longing of the soul, as Christians wrap their lives around the person and cause of Christ, together.

How should church leadership cultivate and celebrate true, biblical fellowship? How should they stay in touch, monthly, with hundreds or thousands of people? One answer is through the ministry of the deacon body. I encourage you, if it does not already exist in your context, to come up with a system by which you can be assured that every member of your church is receiving monthly contacts from someone in leadership at the church. This is not difficult to do when the load is spread among many. If your church does not have a system in place, ask your pastor if he will allow you to create and manage such a system among the deacon body. If you start connecting with people in your church monthly, you will be surprised at their level of commitment. And you will be blessed by the intentional interaction with people who walk the church's journey alongside you.

Widows and Orphans

Psalm 68:5 calls God a "father to the fatherless and a champion of widows." I reflected on this amazing verse of Scripture in a 2019 article in Lifeway's *Deacon Magazine*:

> In biblical times, those with no inheritance were often ostracized; orphans had no family name to claim, and widows lost their economic value the moment they lost their husbands. They were stuck on the bottom rung of the social ladder—the outcast, the pedestrian, the indigent. But the heart of God has always been soft toward the marginalized and forgotten. Isn't it amazing that the God of the ages would rise to be the champion of someone who is defeated by his or

her very identity? Isn't it awesome that this God would add his name
to the nameless and confess his unfailing love to the unloved?[14]

Isn't it humbling that God, in his mercy and because of his great
love for widows and orphans, has invited us to join him in this worthy
ministry of "pure and undefiled religion before God" (James 1:27)?

Orphan care is rising in popularity among the younger generations
of Christ followers, and it's about time. I imagine your church has at least
one family within its fellowship that is involved in orphan care in some
manner: young families adopting from within the county or across
the globe; grandparents or aunts and uncles taking care of children who
are not their own; foster parents connected with a local agency; Child
Protective Services (CPS) employees. Have you considered, as a deacon
body, sponsoring adoptions for couples in your church? Organizing
maintenance or grounds improvement work trips to foster families
or a Christian children's home? Volunteering at pregnancy support
centers? Leading your church to pray for CPS workers and agencies
and other agencies in the same field of work? There are many ways
to be active in orphan care. You just have to be intentional about it.

What about the widows and widowers in your church? Does
your deacon body have a system in place for serving and loving
them? They need your attention. They need your time. Consider
organizing a Valentine's banquet for your church's widows. Take one
or two out to eat with you every few Sundays after church. Take the
widower on a ride one Sunday afternoon with the windows down, or
fishing in the pond out back. Does he or she have special needs with
which you can assist? Transportation to doctors' appointments? A
wheelchair ramp that needs to be built for the front porch? How
about something as simple as washing her car one day or setting up
a visit to just sit and talk for a while?

Serving widows and orphans in and through your local church
body is on the top of God's list when it comes to living out your
faith. So, figure it out. Reach out to them. Serve them. Love them.

Benevolence

Years ago, I served as Music Minister at a church. One Wednesday evening had come upon me rather quickly in the busyness of life and ministry. I was way behind, doing my final walkthrough for choir rehearsal rather frantically with what I estimated would be only seconds to spare. A man wandered in off the streets and caught my eye, but I was too busy to acknowledge him. My associate worship leader Bryan stopped behind me to meet the man, introduce himself, and ask how he could help. He was hungry, and from the looks of him, he may not have eaten much for days. We didn't have much food laying around, but Bryan took him to the kitchen and put together a sandwich and some chips. They sat down together at the hallway table. As the man ate, Bryan shared the gospel with him in a most gracious and loving tone. The man was a professing Christian but had become homeless after some bad occupational and relational choices. I passed by their table several times and overheard the conversation in pieces. I heard them laugh together and saw them talk deeply through what seemed to be serious thoughts. The last time I passed, Bryan had his hands on the man's shoulders, and he was praying over him a prayer of gratitude and expectant faith. The homeless man had his palms open, resting on his knees. In only 30 to 45 minutes, the entire episode was over. The man was gone, and Bryan was back to stuffing music folders. I have no recollection of how choir practice went that night. To this day, I am confident without hesitation that the most important thing that happened that evening was not in my rehearsal room but at that hallway table, and I missed out. Real ministry caught my eye but escaped my heart. Thankfully, Bryan was ready and willing to be the conduit of God's love this man desperately needed that night.

I want you to understand that man could easily have been me or you or one of our family members. Vanessa and I have seen homelessness hit our own family in the past. It is heartbreaking. Here's the thing: life is hard, and people need help. Enter Christian community and the ministry of the deacon. Come to grips with the interminable reality of benevolence needs in the church. No matter where your church is located and no matter what size or shape congregation you serve, benevolence needs will always arise. And God's heart will always be warmed toward the poor and needy:

> If there is a poor person among you, one of your brothers within any of your city gates in the land of the Lord your God is giving you, do not be hardhearted or tightfisted toward your poor brother. (Deuteronomy 15:7)

> If anyone has this world's good and sees a fellow believer in need but withholds compassion from him—how does God's love reside in him? (1 John 3:17)

In short, (a) you will never be benevolent enough to eliminate the need for benevolence in your church/community, and (b) if you have the means and refuse to meet the need, it is not your love for people that is called into question, but your love for God. In every season of your church's life, brothers and sisters will have benevolence needs. There should be an established local network or church ministry strategy for meeting these needs. If your church does not have a benevolence team or a benevolence ministry, the deacons are it. If your church does have such a team or ministry, the deacons should consider working closely together with them to serve the membership and community in this area. When working through a strategy for serving your membership through meeting benevolence needs, here are some questions that may help guide your process:

- Is there a method in place for members of your church to make benevolence requests in confidence? If so, is this well communicated so that your church members know where to go, should a need arise? Perhaps there is a form to fill out online, a request card they can put in a drop box, or a specific point-person (a deacon, maybe) to whom they can speak directly.

+ How does your church receive funds for benevolence needs? Is there a line item in the budget? Is there a designated fund that needs to be monitored? Are the deacons themselves asked to pitch in to help at times? There must be some identifiable financial well from which to draw when requests are made.

+ How will funds be dispersed? Will the requests of non-members be considered? Are cash gifts appropriate in some instances, but not in others? Are there gas or grocery store gift cards on hand at the church office? Who is permitted to give the benevolent gift to the recipient and what record of these gifts is being maintained?

+ How frequently will someone be helped? Is there a percentage cap or a monetary cap on how much the church is able or willing to help in any given instance?

+ Are these policies and procedures clearly set forth somewhere in a church document to reduce the probability of confusion or accidental mishandling?

If no clarity on the ministry currently exists, the deacon body can take the lead in organizing and overseeing benevolent ministries.

Occasional Whole Congregation Service

Be creative in your service. During your next deacons' meeting, schedule a time slot (10–15 minutes) to discuss creative ways you can serve your church body as a whole group. Make it contextual. What areas of your church's body-life provide unique opportunities for you to show them that you love them?

At one church I served as pastor, the deacons came up with the creative idea to take a turn in the rotation of our four Wednesday night cooking teams. Wednesday night meals had become a huge part of our ministry in the community to such a degree that often more people came to Wednesday night activities than Sunday morning services. In our context, the home-cooked meal was the pivot point for this paradigm shift in our Wednesday night reprogramming. Four teams took turns cooking throughout the year, and after 12–18 months, they were tired. So the deacons decided to take one Wednesday night's rotation for each of the teams that year. They fried catfish; they made coleslaw, baked beans, and hushpuppies; and they served every table with a smile on their faces. The real surprise came when families made their way through the line. The normal "$5/person or $10/family" sign was still on the check-in table, but this night it was the attendant's job to say to every family, "There's no cost to you today. The deacons are covering the cost of the meal for you and your family." The response was unbelievably positive. Gratitude poured in, and the people of our community began to see even more that our deacons were sacrificial servants of the church and community.

The last thing you want to hear from a disgruntled church member is, "What do our deacons do, anyway? Take up the offering and pass out the Lord's Supper? Is that it?" The thought should be far from the mind of anyone who is connected to your church. If all the people ever see you doing is gathering in secret corners to make secret plans, or meeting behind closed doors to come up with rules for other people to follow, you're not doing it right. They need to see you serving them.

Deacons are servant leaders. They may not always be out front in their leadership, but they are working diligently behind the scenes. It's not a glamorous job. It's not a position of great authority. By becoming a deacon, you have not been placed over anyone. Rather, you have been placed under the whole church body to lift them up spiritually, physically, and relationally. Deacon, if you are above the people, you are below the office. That's worth writing again: If you are above the people, you are below the office. The more your church members see you serving them, especially as a group, the more they will catch on to the spirit of servanthood your deacon body personifies.

Conclusion

The identity of a Christian within his or her Christian community is a powerful motivator for continued growth in the faith. As Stanley Grenz articulated decades ago, "Our personal stories are never isolated units. They are touched by the stories of other persons and ultimately the story of a larger people of which we are a part. In fact, it is from this larger story that we draw our ideas of value and ultimate meaning. In conversion, we reinterpret our personal story in the light of the story of the Christian community … We are now part of *this* people; we are incorporated into *this* community."[15]

The church is the Body of Christ. Empowered by the Holy Spirit, it is now the physical representation of Christ on the earth until the day Jesus comes again. The church has one prerogative: to carry out Christ's mission in the world. We are to love people with the heart of Jesus, go to people with the feet of Jesus, serve people with the hands of Jesus, and speak to people with the voice of Jesus. As servant leaders, the deacon body in the local church must provide church members with a tangible picture of how this looks. Deacons should embody the story of their Christian family and give their lives in service to "*this* people … *this* community."

I am sure this list is not comprehensive. You should be the experts on service in your own context. However, I do believe that if your deacon body gives devoted attention to these five areas of service—Visitation, Monthly Contacts, Widows and Orphans, Benevolence, and Whole Congregation Service—you will model Christlike servitude to your congregation. Be intentional about this. Set systems in place where needed. Hold each other accountable. When it comes to Jesus's church, you will only serve people to the degree that you sincerely love them like Christ loves them. And sincere, Christlike love is always forged in the fire of selfless service.

Questions for Group Reflection/Discussion

1. What are some ways that your deacon body is currently doing an excellent job serving your church and/or community? Take a few minutes to celebrate those things.

2. Think through each of the five areas of service suggested in this chapter. If you had to pick just one or two, which area(s) needs the most work? What is your next step toward improvement in this area?

3. Is there an area of service that is important to your ministry context but not mentioned in this chapter? If so, what might that be and how can the deacon body begin to engage?

4. Be sure to plan a session when you can talk together as a deacon body about creative ways to serve your church membership. If you have the time, discuss this together right now.

5. Are there people in your church body whom you know are not connected (give specific names, reasons, etc.)? Discuss some ways your deacon body can be intentional in reaching out to them now. How can you make sure this disconnection does not happen again in the future?

Chapter 4

Support the Pastor and Staff

You don't have to be a Bible scholar to see that the seven men of Acts 6:5 were chosen to be supportive of the Apostles' pastoral role. Through servant-minded leadership, these men would support the pastors of their church body. This is especially evidenced in verse 4, "But we will devote ourselves to prayer and to the ministry of the word."

Let's just call it like it is: the Apostles were getting burned out. They were growing weary of the work of the ministry. It was difficult, time-consuming, emotionally draining work. They were unable to keep the main thing the main thing because the supportive things were exhausting them. They needed some men to come alongside them in a supportive role. And that's the role to which the seven were called.

Have you ever served with a pastor who has become burned out? A November 2021 Barna study showed that 38 percent of pastors considered quitting full-time ministry that year. This number represented a 9-point increase from 2020. The percentage was higher among pastors under 40 and among pastors within mainline denominations.[16] I imagine the statistics are the same today, possibly slightly higher. Reasons for pastoral burnout are many, especially in the immediate rebuilding phase of a post-COVID19 world. Emotional distress, decision fatigue, and physical exhaustion compound the normal, everyday pastoral rhythms of leadership, relational attentiveness, calendar-and-time management, prayerful spiritual oversight, soul care, etc. Being a pastor is a rewarding and fulfilling call, but it is a difficult one. Pastors cannot lead and serve the church alone. Thankfully, they don't have to. The third biblical purpose of the deacon is to support the ministry of the pastor and staff in the local church.

I cannot remember when I first read it, but the "can do — should do — must do" leadership paradigm has become a standard in every organizational field over the past several decades. It is a lesson in prioritization and delegation. Trendy and catchy as it is in our day, the principle is ages old. In the opening verses of Acts 6, the Apostles (again, functioning as the pastors of the Jerusalem church) learned that if they were to continue to be successful in God's calling on their lives, they needed to prioritize just two things: the prayer ministry and the preaching/teaching ministry. In James Cartwright Jr.'s words from an article in the inaugural 1970 issue of *Deacon Magazine*, "It is a statement about the wise use of time. The apostles possessed a gift that many in the church could not match; they had been with Jesus. A wise use of their time suggested that they tell this story 'full time.'"[17]

Think about it in terms of your own pastor. Let's call him Pastor Joe. There are a million things Pastor Joe *can* do. He can vacuum floors, paint sheetrock, build a temporary stage for VBS, mow the lawn, print and fold bulletins, and the list goes on. But just because Pastor Joe *can* do something doesn't mean he *should*. Someone else in the church may love to paint walls or mow lawns, and if the pastor performs those tasks himself, he may be robbing a church member of the joy of meaningful service in the church. Also, while Pastor Joe *can* build a temporary stage for VBS, you may not want your children jumping around on a stage he builds. Just sayin'. Maybe carpentry is your pastor's thing and that's great. But if it's not, even though he *can* he probably *shouldn't*.

There are a million things your pastor *can* do but significantly less that he *should* do. Pastors generally should visit church members, serve well in the community, and attend small group and ministry group gatherings throughout the year. But just because he *should* do those things doesn't necessarily mean he *must* do them. Biblically, there are really only two things Pastor Joe *must* do as pastor: preaching/teaching and prayer. Anytime the things he *can* do or the things he *should* do are taking him away from or making him less effective in the two things he *must* do, the church suffers, his family suffers, and he suffers. Matt Smethurst puts the importance of pastoral priorities in proper perspective: "By prioritizing Scripture and prayer, the apostles are choosing to stay focused on the whole church's spiritual welfare, even as they affirm the Hellenists' physical needs. ... A church without deacons may lack health, but a church without biblical preaching cannot exist. There is, in fact, no such thing."[18]

The church needs their pastor to excel in his ministry of the word and in prayer. So, with all the other *can dos* and *should dos* vying for his time and energy, what is the solution? Deacons. By the very nature of the office, deacons make it their business to do things their pastor *can* and/or *should* do. So, as a deacon, these words should never roll off your tongue: "Isn't that something the pastor *can* do? ... Isn't that something the pastor *should* do?" As long as you are a deacon in Christ's church, you will give your time and energy to doing things your pastor *can* and sometimes *should* do. That is the whole point, and it is the joy and the duty of your office.

But the joy of the dual office structure is not only that deacons get to do things on behalf of their pastor. They also get to do things with and for their pastor and his family. I grew up in a pastor's home. My dad was wholeheartedly devoted to the churches and the communities he served. Everything I learned about loving people Jesus's way, I learned by watching my dad. But I can say with confidence that some of the greatest expressions of love I felt outside my own family came from the hearts of deacons who served alongside him. They took me to their homes after church and spent time with me. They came to my ballgames. They gave me high-fives in the school hallways. They stopped by the house to bring us snacks and toys. As a pastor myself now, I know how much that meant to my dad. When the deacon goes out of his way to love on the pastor's family, he displays an immeasurable amount of love and respect for the pastor himself.

When the deacons support the pastor and staff, it is obvious. When they do not support the pastor and staff, it is also obvious. If you want your church to move forward with Christ's mission, storming the gates of Hell with the truth of the gospel, then do this: support your pastor and staff. You don't have to agree with everything they do. You don't even have to like it. But God has called them to lead and you to serve. If you cannot support the mission, vision, and direction of your church staff, you need to talk it out with them. And if the matter is irreconcilable, you need to consider quietly stepping down as a deacon.

In *The Deacon Ministry Handbook*, Paul Badgett argues that the pastor and deacon should have such a close relationship, such healthy biblical community, that friendship is special between them. "Too many pastors can identify with the psalmist David, who wrote, 'No man cared for my soul,' (Ps. 142:4 KJV). ... The Bible [also] says, 'A friend loves at all times' (Prov. 17:17). The deacon should always be a true friend to his pastor."[19] In the context of friendship, we learn to trust one another and listen to one another. Every pastor needs faithful men in his life whom he can trust not only with the work of the ministry but the care of his own soul.

Here are a few areas of suggestion for supporting your pastor and staff. These are not meant to be comprehensive or exhaustive but may be a good place to start. These suggestions are born not only from Scripture, but also from my own experience as a pastor's son, church staff member, pastor, and denominational servant. Take these and run with them if you'd like. Make it your goal to ensure that your pastor, staff, and their families know that they have your love and support.

Intentional Encouragement

Do you know who (usually) is your pastor's greatest discourager? Himself. Every week he invests 16–20 hours, on average, into praying over, studying for, and preparing one 35-minute sermon. (Co-vocational pastors are usually able to get it done in about 6–10 hours every week. I believe God gives a special dispensation of grace to those who serve as co-vocational pastors. They are my heroes. The tip of the spear.) Each Sunday morning, your pastor stands before Christ's people and pours his heart out. And every Sunday afternoon he replays in his mind all the things he hoped to say differently, the illustrations he blundered, and/or the feeling of disconnection between pulpit and pew. Most pastors I know do not need help being discouraged. Sadly, however, such help regularly finds them.

You may be surprised (or you may not) that your pastor and church staff take a lot of negativity from church members each week. Every Sunday the worship leader hears about songs some don't like and instruments of which some don't approve. Every Wednesday your student and children's ministry leaders are bombarded by parents who missed a deadline, are concerned about the lack of security in the department, or would rather their child not be around Mrs. Smith's child. Every Monday your administrative assistants are emailed about misprints or misspellings in the bulletin. And you probably can't imagine the times of day people call your pastor or drop by his house just to "speak their mind."

As a pastor, I had a conversation one day that left me discouraged, drained, and dejected. I felt like a complete and total failure. Thankfully, an older deacon stopped by my office only a few days later. He knocked on the door, eased into one of the chairs across my desk, and simply asked, "Well, how's my pastor doing?"

And for about 30 minutes, he just affirmed me and encouraged me. He will never know how timely that support was, how critical it was to my ministry.

Deacon, your pastor and church staff desperately need your encouragement. They need you to take time out of your day and intentionally connect with them, to say that you love them and support them. Their young families hear a lot of things and see a lot of things that could possibly make them despise church for the rest of their lives. You must counteract that. You must reach out to the families of church staff members and encourage them. Even when it's nothing more than, "You know we love your dad/mom, and he's/she's doing a great job."

One faithful church member shared about his desire to be a regular encourager for his pastor: "I decided I would never criticize my pastor. I wanted him to hear positive feedback and words of affirmation from me. I wanted him to smile when he saw me coming, knowing I was coming to bless him in some way. Encouraged pastors are better pastors for the churches they serve."[20]

Does your pastor smile when he sees you coming? I am sure there are things your pastor and staff members do of which you disapprove. That's because they're human. So are you. So, push those things aside and focus on the things you can support. It is not your job to criticize or belittle the pastor and staff. It is your job to support and encourage them.

Wise Counsel

Bro. Ray was a kind and thoughtful deacon. He had earned the respect of the congregation and the community by being a man full of integrity and wisdom for many decades. One evening, I drove around back and found him in his garden, picking peas. After a particularly difficult week, I had a decision to make that I dreaded facing alone. I knelt down beside him and poured my heart out, right there in the fourth dirt row. He took me inside and we cried together for a while. His wife Yvonne made up a fresh batch of sweet tea. He did not help me solve the problem that day, but he listened and helped me cry. He and Yvonne prayed over me and sent me off. As it turned out, that's exactly what I needed. A few days later, Bro. Ray showed up in my office and poured into me some of the most godly, sincere wisdom that I have ever received. I don't believe anyone else could have offered the wise counsel he shared with me that day. Better than anyone else in that moment of crisis, Ray knew the story, the context, the people involved, and the way the decision burdened my soul. He walked with God and allowed himself to be a conduit of the spiritual wisdom I needed.

Your pastor likely has pastor friends, associational leaders, and denominational networkers he can call at the drop of a hat for encouragement and counsel. But there are many times your pastor needs advice from someone who shares his ministerial context. That's you. Be the kind of deacon your pastor knows he can turn to for good, biblical advice, never in arrogance or pride, but always with a measure of humility and genuine respect. Be the kind of deacon that knows when your pastor needs you to help solve a problem, and when he just needs you to help him cry and help him pray.

Pastoral Care

Of the seven deacons called in Acts 6, only two are ever mentioned again in the Bible: Stephen and Philip. Steven was a man "full of grace and power," and when he defended the faith publicly his opponents "were unable to stand against" him (Acts 6:8–10). Acts 6–7 tell the story of Stephen's boldness in preaching the gospel to the Jerusalem Jews. The episode ends with Deacon Stephen's stoning, the first Christian martyr. Oh, to have the faith and the courage of Stephen, the faithful, fearless, servant-hearted preaching deacon!

Acts 7 ends with Stephen's martyrdom, and then next chapter begins with Philip's shining moment. Here, a table-waiting deacon became a faith-filled personal evangelist. He stood against the façade of Simon's sorcery and then led the Ethiopian eunuch to Christ. Philip was an evangelist, a preacher, and a timely instrument in the hand of God. In Acts 21, the Apostle Paul and his missionary team journeyed from Tyre, through Ptolemais, then to Caesarea. They were tired, weary, and spiritually and emotionally drained. Philip had seen that look before on the faces of the apostles in Acts 6. He knew the burden that pastors and missionaries share, and he knew they needed relief, encouragement, and simple rest. So, the deacon evangelist Philip opened his home to them. For several days, Philip and his family cared for them. They ministered to them. They cleaned the missionaries' clothes, washed their feet, served them meals, and let them rest. With the flip of a page, Philip the fearless evangelist deacon became Philip the humble, selfless hospitable deacon. What a great blessing he was to Paul as he allowed himself to be used of the Lord in a moment of much needed pastoral care.

Your pastor and church staff try very hard to be at the bedside of people in need, write notes of sympathy, make phone calls of encouragement, and keep up with the latest details of each church member's latest dramatic saga. And you help them with this. They try to keep up with you, their deacons, to love on you, encourage you, invest in you, and be there for you when you need them most. This is their pastoral care to their flock, and it is a genuine joy. But who does the work of pastoral care for them?

Who cares for your pastor and your staff members when they are sick, distraught, or facing a timely burden or difficult decision? You do, deacon. Pastoring can be so lonely at times: you pour your whole life into other people and when you are empty and dry, no one pours back into you. That is, unless you have a great deacon body who knows how to care for their pastor. My friend Mark Dance has said it well, "Your church is more than a job to your pastor, and he should be more than an employee to you."[21]

Think practically. How can you ensure that your pastor and

church staff are receiving the same pastoral care that they are giving to the church body? How can the deacon body pour into them, love on them, and shepherd them while they are investing their lives in so many? How can you, like Philip, be used of the Lord in moments of much needed pastoral care, for your pastor and church staff?

Public Endorsement

The "honeymoon" principle is so true. The first six months to one year of a pastor's tenure are generally fun and exciting. But it does not take long for people to begin compiling complaints against him, whether they keep these complaints to themselves or share them with others. The congregation soon finds out that their pastor is not perfect, as they have presumed, and that he intends to make some changes in the church that they may or may not have been ready to receive. The pastor is new and has little or no relational capital in the congregation. The deacon, however, has likely been around for decades and is seen as one from among the congregation, of good reputation, full of the Spirit and wisdom, and able to do the work (Acts 6:3). The deacon can and should leverage his relational equity to help the pastor succeed in the direction God has called him to lead. Deacons need to publicly endorse their pastor and their pastor's biblical vision for the church.

In every church I served as pastor or interim pastor, I told the deacons that, when the doors were closed, if they thought it, I needed them to say it. I made it my practice to share plans, changes, and directional shifts with the deacons first. If it didn't sound right with them, it most likely wouldn't with some in the congregation either. I needed a safe place to test the waters, and some trusted voices who would ask probing questions. Inside that room, we could talk about anything. We could disagree openly if we disagreed lovingly. As a result, countless plans I have made through the years were changed or redirected thanks to the thoughtful and supportive voices of my deacons behind closed doors. I would always tell them,

"If you disagree with something, we all need to know it in here. So, if you think it, say it." But at the end of the meeting, whatever was decided, we walked out with one mind and one voice. Even when a deacon did not like a particular decision or direction, that deacon was expected to be 100 percent behind it. Private pushback. Public endorsement. And the rest of the deacons knew it was their job to hold each other accountable to this.

Deacon, if you have a complaint against your pastor, take it to him privately. It is never appropriate for a deacon to publicly criticize his pastor's leadership. Two offices are given to the church, and if they are pulling in different directions, you can expect a split down the middle. If the church does not sense unity between the deacons and staff, implosion is soon to come.

Additionally, take every opportunity possible to brag on your pastor and staff. Not patronizingly. Just think of those qualities you love and appreciate in your pastor and hold them high to your friends and church members. Think about leveraging your relational equity on the pastor's behalf. The more your membership hears public praise for the leadership coming from the deacons' mouths, the more they will think positively about the vision and direction of your church. Publicly endorse your pastor and church staff. Be their cheerleader. Always remember this rule: public praise, private pushback. This is the only recipe for forward direction in the church.

Conclusion

My oldest son played the bass in our church praise band. He was a young teenager at the time but was extremely gifted in musical ability. One of my deacons, Bruce, played the electric guitar beside him. Forty years split the middle between them, but they were the best of friends. They texted each other and pulled jokes on each other. Sometimes during rehearsal or even during a church service, I wasn't sure if I needed to correct my son or my deacon. They were quite the pair. My son knew this man loved him with the love of Christ. That was almost ten years ago, and my son still remembers the intentionality with which Bruce invested in him, served him, and supported him.

When I answered the call to my first senior pastorate, my youngest son was pulled from the city and thrust into the country at a very awkward stage of life. He wanted to shoot guns and be a country boy like the other kids his age, but he had a bit of a learning curve to overcome. As it turns out, his dad (that's me) could rip lips in the stocked ponds like a pro but couldn't shoot his way out of a wet paper bag. One of my deacons connected with him and they struck up a friendship that, I think, surprised them both. He had my son over at his house once or twice a month and let him shoot chickens, clean them, and bring them home. My son loved this deacon, and he knew that the deacon loved him. To this day he still remembers the way this man and his wife approved of him, supported him, and loved him.

Sometimes the simplest little things you do as a deacon are what mean the most to your pastor and staff. Maybe you can show your support in other creative ways. Maybe it's a double date with your wife and the pastor and his wife. Maybe it's a simple, handwritten card in the mail. Maybe it's a stop by the office just to say, "I love you, and I'm proud of you."

In their 2017 book *Lift Your Pastor*, Michael Lewis and Andy Spencer draw from the deep well of their special friendship, as a pastor and his deacon, to offer timely wisdom for local churches. The book offers ten practical ways a deacon can support his pastor as he lifts the load of ministry, encourages him, affirms him, prays for him, helps him manage time, rallies others to his support, and more.[22] The book is a wonderful resource for deacons who hope to leverage their time and relationships to help their pastor be successful. However you go about supporting your pastor and staff, be sure they never have to assume your support. Show it to them. Tell it to them. Make sure everyone else knows, too. Don't leave room for your pastor or church staff to doubt your love and support. Make sure they hear it, see it, and feel it.

Questions for Group Reflection/Discussion

1. In what ways were the seven men in Acts 6 supporting their pastors?

2. What are some ways you currently show support to your pastor and staff? What are some creative ways you can begin to do this better?

3. Does your pastor or his family assume your support, or are they assured of it?

4. How can you begin to develop the kind of relationship with your church leadership that would invite them to ask for your counsel/advice?

5. Do you have a plan in place for the pastoral care of your pastor and church staff?

Chapter 5

Protect the Peace

Have you ever been to Israel? For a Christian living in the occident, it is one of the most spiritually rewarding trips you can ever make. The Bible comes to life in Israel as you walk the ancient paths of our faith. You can lean against the columns of the temple in Capernaum, sit in Caiaphas's pit, walk the streets of Tel Dan, squeeze through Hezekiah's tunnel, pray at the Western Wall, kneel in the Garden of Gethsemane, swim in Gideon's spring, float in the Dead Sea, boat ride on the Sea of Galilee, and so much more. Watch out for peddlers, though. They are everywhere and they know how to tug on your Christian heartstrings at just the right moment and sell you a fake relic at a high price.

Thankfully, the first time I travelled to Israel our tour guide was also a registered archeologist. I desperately wanted to bring home a first century oil lamp. He helped me, from site to site and shop to shop, find authentic pieces and good deals. Admittedly, I still paid more than I anticipated, but I got that oil lamp I so desperately wanted. It travelled home with me on the plane, wrapped in packing bubbles and secured by dozens of pieces of packing paper. Back home, in my office, I secured it in a display case and set it on a shelf where it rests alone to this day. Other than me and my wife, no one on this side of the Atlantic has touched that oil lamp. It's too precious to me, and it's extremely delicate. So, I put measures in place to protect it.

Most things that are precious are also delicate. Such is the case with unity and peace in the church body. As you read the New Testament epistles, it is almost daunting how much ink and space is expended to address the issues of keeping the peace and building or protecting unity. Apparently, Christians in the first century were real people with real problems, too. Their everyday struggles, varying life stages, and clashing personalities gave rise to a number of disruptions in the first-century church.

Other than the gospel itself, the most precious possession a church can have is unity. In John 17, on the night of his betrayal, the Lord Jesus prayed an extended audible prayer while his remaining eleven disciples listened in. Jesus begins by praying for himself, anticipating the moment when the Father will restore the glory to him that he had known from eternity past. In verse six he shifts and begins praying for "the people you gave me," namely, his disciples. He prays for their completed joy, for protection from evil, and for a sanctified future ministry. Then, in verse twenty he shifts again, this time praying "not only for these but also for those who believe in me through their word." In other words, he's praying for me and you and anyone else who has heard the gospel and believed in Jesus. Jesus prayed for us, out loud, the night of his betrayal, there beside the Kidron Valley on his way to the Garden of Gethsemane. What did he pray? "May they all be one, as you, Father, are in me and I am in you. May they also be [made one] in us, so that the world may believe you sent me," (John 17:21). Don't miss the words "so that." In a single sentence, Jesus directly tied the effectiveness of our gospel witness to our unity.

The degree of our Christian unity will, in some way, correspond to the degree to which non-Christians believe the gospel of Jesus Christ. You know as well as I do that unity is sacred, precious, and delicate. If you have it, you know how special it is. If you don't have it, you long for nothing more. Unity is not uniformity; it doesn't mean we all have to look the same, speak the same, vote the same, and act the same. Unity is not unanimity, that we would require

100 percent agreement on every decision all the time. Unity is a sanctified, grace-filled ethos of biblical togetherness; unity means we acknowledge our differences and genuinely love and serve each other through those differences while we move forward together in Great Commission advance.

In Acts 6, these seven deacons were first called to service because "there arose a complaint" (Acts 6:1)—four words no deacon ever wants to hear. It should be noted that this disunity surfaced in a season of growth for the church. The dispute came "as the disciples were increasing in number." Church conflict is real because people's problems are real. Even in a growing church, unity is precious because conflict is real. Conflict does not always mean a church is unhealthy. And as we'll see throughout this chapter, conflict often presents opportunity for even greater health. In fact, healthy conflict navigation is a sign of church health: "Healthy churches experience conflict, navigate it in healthy, biblical ways, and become stronger on the other side of it."[23] Matt Smethurst calls attention to long-term danger behind the short-term problem: "Of the many lessons for deacons from Acts 6, perhaps most overlooked is their strategic role in preserving congregational unity. The seven weren't merely deployed to solve a food problem. Food was the occasion, sure, but it wasn't the deepest problem. The deepest problem was a sudden threat to church unity."[24] When the problem was solved in the Jerusalem church, through the faithful service of deacons, the church experienced continued growth and Great Commission advancement (Acts 6:7). That's the goal. When deacons serve well, presenting problems become springboards for church growth and gospel advance.

Isn't it woefully ironic that deacons were first chosen and ordained as the solution to conflict in the church, but some deacons in our day are the source of conflict in the church? Deacons should never be instigators of, or even a part of, church conflict. Such engagement is antithetical to their very existence. Instead, when conflict arises, deacons should lead the way toward resolution. From day one, deacons have been peacekeepers. The nature of their service to the church demands their readiness to resolve conflicts and redirect people to the cause of Christ and the mission of the church. The fourth and final biblical purpose of the deacon is to be a peacekeeper. To be a deacon on purpose, you must constantly labor to protect the peace.

Here are five ways that you, as a deacon, can protect the peace within your church body.

Defuse Conflict

The fuse is lit. Emotions are high. Careless words are flung. Accusations are made. And there you are, strategically positioned right in the middle of it all. As a keeper of the peace, it is your job to defuse this situation before it explodes. These things often happen when you least expect them. Such conversations are born in the hearts of disgruntled church members, incubated in the closed circles of secret conversations, and then taken home atop the carpeted floors of church hallways or in the circled chairs of Sunday School discussion times. Your deacon body is dispersed among the church body during all regularly scheduled and special activities. You are representatives of the church's leadership on the front lines of interpersonal spiritual warfare. Be ever ready.

How can you defuse such a situation before it explodes? Here are some suggestions:

- Step into the conversation. Sometimes, when you overhear a tense conversation, if you simply step into that conversation, the negative talk will stop. You may not have to say anything, or you may have to turn the conversation around positively. And you have my permission (as if you need it) to stand there awkwardly until someone else leaves. You probably didn't resolve the conflict, I know. But you did defuse it, at least for now. After that conversation, you can ask the main dissenters to talk with you privately so that you can better understand their concerns.

"Mrs. Sally, it seemed like you and Mrs. Jean were upset about something earlier this morning. Is everything okay?"

+ Encourage Christians to practice the guidelines for conflict resolution as set forth in Matthew 18:15–17. If you are not sure what these steps look like, ask your pastor now, during a time of peace, about the process. Matthew 18:15–17 is Jesus's plan for conflict resolution in the church. When anyone brings a conflict to you, your first question must be, "Have you talked to him/her about this directly?" If you start anywhere else, well-meaning as you are, you have told Jesus Christ that your plan for conflict resolution is better than his. Take some time as a deacon body to work through this passage and decide together how to follow these biblical steps amidst real-time scenarios in your church.

+ When the concern is an accusation against church leadership, listen carefully and cautiously. Be very careful receiving an accusation against a pastor in the church (see 1 Timothy 5:19). If there is any substance to a concern against your pastor, after asking if he or she has spoken directly to the pastor about it and taken a witness to the pastor (Matthew 18:15–17) with no resolution, ask the church member to refrain from discussing it with anyone else while you bring it to the attention of the appropriate person. Then you should talk to the pastor about the issue and possibly the deacon body, too.

+ Sometimes, the concern is based on false or incomplete data. Correct false information in a gentle way. Learn to speak the truth in love (Ephesians 4:15).

+ Sometimes the stirring conflict has a simple solution. How can you suggest or make a simple change that will solve the problem immediately? The Acts 6 deacons put on their aprons and served tables. That solved the problem. What can you do to roll up your sleeves and serve the conflict away?

Correct, Reprove, Admonish

"That's just not true," I told the middle-aged woman as I stood beside her hospital bed. "And now I'd like you to call everyone you've talked to about this and correct the false information you've spread." I was visiting her in the hospital after she experienced a mild heart problem. When a church member is on her back in a hospital bed, it is often easy for her to assume a level of sympathetic kindness from her visitor. But when her complaint about some decisions I had made was tested against the truth, it just did not measure up. "But I've heard from several people!" she insisted. And I responded, "Well, what you're saying is false. And I love you enough to tell you the truth: that by repeating this, you are spreading false rumors and disrupting the good fellowship of our church." She called her friends that afternoon, from her hospital bed, and corrected the false information they had been spreading.

Another scenario did not end so positively. The second week of my pastoral leadership at one church, a deacon's wife called me at home. She began to talk about several church members she thought I should be careful around, accusing them of things ranging from flirting and adultery to drug usage and anger mismanagement. I stopped her two minutes into the conversation. "Mrs. Smith … Mrs. Smith, I'm sorry, but this sounds like gossip, and I really don't want to be part of it. Is there something else you want to talk about?" She hung up the phone immediately, then she and her husband set out to ruin me in the church. Within several months, they had caused quite the stir and it ended in their own unceremonious departure.

Protecting the peace often means confronting falsehoods and admonishing sin with an unwavering insistence. The people in your church family are real people with real problems, just like you. They are all on a journey toward Christlikeness, just like you. And some have a long road ahead of them. Some of the most meaningful teaching moments happen not in a classroom, but in a hallway. Not from a pulpit on a stage, but from a recliner in a living room. Not from behind a megaphone, but from behind a telephone.

The people under your deacon body's care are not to be placated in their unrighteousness. They are to be loved and challenged toward godliness. Paul wrote to young Timothy: "All Scripture is inspired by God, and is profitable for teaching, for rebuking, for correcting, for training in righteousness, so that the man of God may be complete, equipped for every good work" (2 Timothy 3:16–17). In his 2022 book *Leading Church Revitalization*, Mark Hallock comments on this passage and the importance of holding one another accountable to the biblical witness in general: "Laying our conflict before Scripture provides an opportunity for the Word of God to grow us, to teach us, to bring reproof, to bring correction, and to train us in the ways of righteousness as individuals and as a church body. Only the Spirit of God working through the Word of God can do this."[25]

It is not our duty to avoid conflict, but to humbly embrace the "opportunity for growth" it presents.[26] It is the responsibility of every deacon (and every Christian, honestly) to confront the unrighteousness or untruthfulness of church members when such an opportunity arises. In doing this, you become a protector of the peace and an instrument of righteousness.

Give Others the Benefit of the Doubt

It is all too easy to come to quick conclusions. But as a deacon, you must refuse to make up your mind about an issue before you hear both sides. Proverbs 18:13 offers timely counsel: "The one who gives an answer before he listens—this is foolishness and disgrace for him." Any time an accusation is made, deacon, you must listen to every side of the argument before formulating opinions or judgments. This is crucial to keeping peace in the church body.

Once, in a talk on self-discipline and Christian holiness, I heard Jimmy Draper say, "We are all capable of the worst evils we can possibly imagine." That stuck with me. Over the years I have watched many of my Christian leader friends fall into moral and ethical sins that sent shock waves across their communities of faith. Sin is pervasive and persuasive. Apart from walking in the Spirit, every one of us is susceptible to its lure, and most of us are more susceptible in one area than in others. Another has said it like this: "A wise man or woman is someone who knows that there is no sin of which he or she is not capable."[27] This is important to note because most of us peacekeepers are inclined to give our hearts to the first thing we hear, especially if the accusation comes from someone we know, love, and trust. But even they are entirely capable of the evils they attribute to another. If you are to be a deacon who keeps the peace, you cannot give your heart to the first thing you hear. As you help church members walk through Matthew 18:15–17, resolve to listen to all sides of a conflict or do not involve yourself at all.

Keep in mind that deciding who is wrong and who is right is not always a matter of your concern. You are not a judge but a peacekeeper. Often, there's not much you can do when a complaint comes to you. Help the Christian redirect offense to opportunity: "I'm so sorry to hear this, and I can only imagine how you feel. Tell me, how do you think God is going to use this moment/season to shape and mold you into the Christian man (or woman) he wants you to be?" Or, "Five or ten years from now, what do you want to say was true of you today while you walked through this season?" With a single question, you have diverted the conversation away from the danger of interpersonal warfare and toward the opportunity of personal spiritual growth. No matter who is the offender and who is the offended, the goal is always forgiveness and reconciliation on both "sides." That leads us nicely to the next way you can actively help protect the peace as a deacon in Jesus's church.

Seek Restoration in All Conflicts

Having pastored in a very small East Texas town, I am well aware of the temptation to think that some conflicts are irreconcilable because they run generations deep. However, I can say from experience that this is only true when people deny the power of the Holy Spirit as he works through the gospel of Jesus Christ for the glory of the Father in heaven. As another has said, "We can't change a heart, only the Spirit can, so we want to assume the best of our brothers and sisters. So instead of painting this bleak picture that there's no hope for this person, we should be saying, 'There is hope, because the Lord God is at work in this individual.'"[28]

In my relational work throughout the community, I discerned a deeply rooted conflict between two families in a certain Texas town. I had recently led members of each family to Christ, and I was discipling the dads privately, personally. I longed for the day when they would be faithful members of the same church. As I mined their deep-seated conflict over several months, I came to understand that neither family could point to a specific occasion or instance in which their conflict began. They just, for whatever reason, didn't like each other (I found out later the root of the conflict was decades deep, between the parents of the parents). Each family began to attend worship services and joined the church, although they sat on opposite sides of the worship center.

One Sunday, after preaching a sermon on reconciliation and loving togetherness in the body of Christ, I saw the dads make eye contact and nod heads on their way out the door. The next Sunday, during the welcome time of the service, while everyone was shaking hands with the people around them, I watched from the stage as the husband and wife of each family walked across the worship center to meet each other in the middle. Amid the shakes of a hundred hands around them, the husbands and wives embraced each other with a warm hug and pulled away with a smile. Two weeks later, I was invited to one of their birthday parties at a local restaurant. Vanessa and I walked in a little late and made our way to the back room where I was pleasantly surprised to see the two families sitting at the same table together, laughing and enjoying one another's company.

They were more than reconciled. They had become friends, and they still are to this day.

Restoration is always possible through the work of the Holy Spirit. Deacon, if you don't believe this, who will? Do not write off some conflicts as irreconcilable. Pray for healing in the power of the Holy Spirit. Work with the offended and the offenders. Cling to the promises of God's Word. And be ever ready to speak a word of encouragement or exhortation when the timing is right.

Notify the Pastor or Staff

Sometimes, it is best not to burden your pastor or church staff if an issue/conflict is relatively small, relatively contained, and quickly resolved. Other times, it is vital for church leadership to have a working knowledge of the situation. This is not about gossip or hearsay. It's about protecting your pastor's blindside. Imagine your pastor walking into a deacon meeting heartbroken and dismayed because he just learned of a dissolving marriage or a major conflict in the church. He bears his heart to you and says, "If I had known this was happening, I could have prayed for them or counseled them through it." And there you are, leaning back in your seat, thinking, "I knew about this three months ago but didn't say anything."

Informing your pastor of conflict or potential conflict in the church is as simple as, "Pastor, I'm not even sure if this is true, but I thought you'd want to know that _____. I will not talk to anyone about it, and every time I have heard the rumor, I have encouraged our people not to gossip and, instead, to pray in secret about the matter. But I thought you might want to know in case you run into this person or see/hear something concerning."

The last thing you want is for your pastor to be blindsided by a boiling conflict within the church about which you had previous knowledge. Hebrews 13:17 says your pastor "keeps watch over your souls as one who will give an account." It is his job and his joy to labor in soul care for the spiritual health of individual church members and the body as a whole. But he cannot prayerfully labor over something about which he is unaware. In *On Being A Deacon*, Noble, Thistlethwaite, Von Kaenel, and Hallock encourage deacons to "keep the pulse of the church as the eyes and ears of the pastors within the body."[29] Deacons may primarily be the pastor's hands and feet, but they can also be his eyes and ears. But how much do you tell the pastor, and when? Here are some principles to help guide whether or not you should share information about a conflict with your pastor:

- If the conflict involves more than two or three people, always notify your pastor. By "involves," I mean that those people are either actively engaged in the conflict or are actively conversing about it. Your pastor may not be able to do anything about it immediately, but it will be good for him to be aware that the conflict is brewing. It may save him from conversational embarrassment or from stoking the flames of a fire that he does not yet see.

- You, deacon, should do everything in your power to help resolve the issue in accordance with Matthew 18:15–17. Ask, "How can I protect the peace by serving the membership in this situation?" "Is there something I can do, right now, that will help resolve this issue?" That's your job, as a peacekeeper. When you notify the pastor of an ongoing conflict, you are not necessarily handing it off to him. As long as the pastor believes it appropriate, continue to help the members resolve the issue.

- If you have attempted to help the offended parties seek reconciliation biblically, but it has not been effective, or if they are resisting reconciliation, then tell your pastor. Even if it is between only two people in the church, if they are not willing to work toward resolution, seek your pastor's advice and counsel in how to proceed.

- ✦ If it involves a moral failure or any kind of action that affects the body-life of the whole congregation, tell your pastor. Moral failures do not fizzle out and they do not stay quiet. Your pastor needs to know.

- ✦ Any action involving mishandling of church funds or church property, even if only one or two people know about it, needs to be directed to your pastor immediately.

- ✦ Any conflict at all that involves a church staff member or another deacon must go directly and immediately to your pastor. Division in the official ranks is a recipe for implosion, and it must be handled quickly and carefully.

- ✦ Do everything in your power not to bring conflicts to the attention of your pastor on Sunday morning before the worship service. I promise, if it is a conflict at 9:00 a.m., it will be a conflict at 12:15 p.m. He needs to focus on the worship service. Help protect his spirit and his focus by waiting for a more appropriate time.

Remember, you are an extension of your pastor's ministry. Sometimes that means being feet that go and hands that serve. Sometimes it means being eyes that see and ears that listen. When the deacon body is functioning properly, keeping the peace of the congregation on the front of their minds, the pastor can become aware of rising conflicts before they cause irreparable damage within the church. Part of protecting the peace means notifying the pastor or church staff when appropriate. If you are unsure, always err on the side of informing the pastor. Too much communication can be unnecessary and time-consuming, for sure. But too little communication can be detrimental to the body-life of the church. Perhaps this is why the apostles directed the church to select men who were full of the Spirit *and wisdom* (Acts 6:3). Be a man full of wisdom, and leverage that wisdom appropriately when discerning how and when to inform your pastor about conflict in the church.

Conclusion

Dietrich Bonhoeffer was arguably one of the most inspiring and influential Christian theologians of the twentieth century. A German pastor and professor in America, he left the safety and security of the West during World War II to travel home to Germany where he would share the gospel with and minister to his own people. There, he was eventually imprisoned and executed for his Christian witness. But in a world of war, Bonhoeffer knew something about Christian peace. Commenting on the seventh beatitude in Matthew 5:9, he wrote:

> The followers of Jesus have been called to peace. When he called them they found their peace, for he is their peace. But now they are told that they must not only have peace but make it. And to that end they renounce all violence and tumult. In the cause of Christ nothing is to be gained by such methods. His kingdom is one of peace, and the mutual greeting of his flock is a greeting of peace. His disciples keep the peace by choosing to endure suffering themselves rather than inflict it on others. They maintain fellowship where others would break it off. They renounce all self-assertion, and quietly suffer in the face of hatred and wrong. In so doing they overcome evil with good, and establish the peace of God in the midst of a world of war and hate. But nowhere will that peace be more manifest than where they meet the wicked in peace and are ready to suffer at their hands. The peacemakers will carry the cross with their Lord, for it was on the cross that peace was made. Now that they are partners in Christ's work of reconciliation, they are called the sons of God as he is the Son of God.[30]

As peacekeepers, deacons "carry the cross of their Lord." In so doing they become partners with Christ in the "work of reconciliation." There, in that sacred space of peacekeeping, they are rightfully called the sons of God.

Peace within the Body of Christ is about more than functional necessity; it's about identity. It's about walking worthy of our calling in Christ. Consider Paul's exhortation to the church in Ephesus: "Therefore I, the prisoner of the Lord, urge you to live worthy of the calling you have received, with all humility and gentleness, with patience, bearing with one another in love, making every effort to keep the unity of the Spirit through the bond of peace," (Ephesians 4:1–3). Patience … bearing with one another … making every effort. The very thought of it all assumes that conflict is around every corner. Keeping the peace within the church body is something that takes determination, consistency, and long-suffering. It is the high calling of every deacon. To be a deacon on purpose, you must be willing to put forth the prayerful and faith-filled effort, energy, and time required to be a dutiful protector of peace.

Questions for Group Reflection/Discussion

1. How did the service of the seven men in Acts 6:1–7 keep the peace within their church body?

2. Are there any conflicts stirring in your church currently that might endanger its peace and good fellowship? How have you helped (or how can you help) address those issues biblically?

3. Walk through Matthew 18:15–17 together and work to agree on what that process looks like in your church.

4. Has there been a time when you, as a deacon, have acted against this important purpose of keeping the peace within your church? (That is to say, have you ever been part of the problem rather than part of the solution?) Confess it now and seek forgiveness and reconciliation within your deacon body. Watch and learn first-hand how the love of Jesus covers every offense and brings reconciliation among the saints.

5. Talk together through the bullet points under the subheading "Defuse Conflict," on pages 58–59. Can you give a personal example that illustrates one of these bullet points?

Chapter 6

Character and Purpose

Who is qualified to serve as a deacon? What are those qualifications, and why do they matter? Our case study for
A Deacon On Purpose has been Acts 6:1–7. As evident in verse
three, six qualifications were listed for the Jerusalem congregation's
consideration.

(1) "Select from among you." Those chosen to serve in this
official capacity were from among the congregation. They were
known and actively involved in the body-life of the church. This was
not a popularity contest, but the seven must have been a known,
recognized, and active part of the church body.

(2) "Seven men." The Jerusalem congregation was to select
"seven men." Much argument has been made in favor of godly,
servant-hearted women holding the office of deacon, with demon-
strable historical precedent and growing popularity in twenty-
first century Baptist circles. In his 2021 book *Deacons: How they
Serve and Strengthen the Church*, Matt Smethurst lays out a chari-
table and honest biblical case for both convictions, explaining the
typical reasons churches believe that the office of deacon is and
is not open to qualified women.[31] I disagree with Smethurst's
conclusion, remaining unconvinced by biblical arguments in the
affirmative. I'm convinced that an all-male diaconate represents
the most straight-forward reading of the biblical texts. However,
it's worth mentioning that some of my most trusted, respected,

and theologically conservative Baptist friends come to a different conviction on the issue. Godly, servant-hearted women holding the office of deacon is not a hill on which I would even remotely consider dying. But inasmuch as Acts 6:1–7 is foundational for the office of deacon, at least in Acts 6:3 the qualification for an all-male diaconate in the first-century Jerusalem church is difficult to deny.

(3) "Of good reputation." Not all actively present males would qualify. They must have a good reputation. That is to say, the men must be both well-known and well-respected. Celebrity and prominence were not the issue. Faithfulness to Christ was. The Greek word here is *martureo*, the root word for our modern word "martyr," most commonly translated as "witness" in the New Testament. The men must be well-known as faithful witnesses of the gospel of Jesus Christ, in both word and action, whatever the cost. Their Christian walk needed to match their Christian talk.

(4) "Full of the Spirit." Modern day Christians often have a difficult time understanding exactly what is meant by "full of the Holy Spirit." The congregation of Acts 6, however, knew exactly what to look for. In Acts 2:4, the 120 believers were all "filled with the Holy Spirit" and began to supernaturally and powerfully testify to the gospel of Jesus Christ in other known languages. They shared the gospel one-on-one all day with those who drew near, and three thousand souls were baptized. In Acts 4:31, the church held a prayer meeting during which the ground was physically shaken, and they were all "filled with the Holy Spirit" and began to share the gospel even more boldly than before in the face of persecution. The Jerusalem congregation was to look for consistent, devoted, emboldened, spirit-led gospel witness in the men they would select to serve them as deacons. And they all knew very well what that looked like.

(5) "Full ... of wisdom." The difference between knowledge and wisdom is important. Knowledge is about what you know. Wisdom is about what you do with what you know. These men were not just

to know things about Christ and the way of God. They were to appropriately apply that knowledge in their daily walk with Jesus. Holding the office of deacon would require the proper and prudent application of biblical knowledge. They needed to be "full ... of wisdom."

(6) "Who we can appoint to this duty." The men needed to be able and willing. The Jerusalem church's deacons would not be sitting in a back room making decisions for others to follow. They would be actively, consistently, selflessly serving the church body.

The six qualifications of Acts 6:3 are pretty compelling, if you ask me. In a single sentence, the apostles gave their Jerusalem congregation six clear, distinct credentials. And honestly, it's really not all that complicated of a list. In their 2019 book, *On Being a Deacon*, Pastor Mark Hallock and several of his deacons boiled the issue of qualification down to 5 simple marks: Love for God, Love for People, Humility, Flexibility, and Sacrifice.[32] It's not more complicated than that.

Another passage informs what is commonly understood as a list of qualifications for deacons: 1 Timothy 3:8–13. I maintain that this passage is not as much a checklist for qualifications as it is a description of character traits expected in both those who are under consideration and those who continue to serve. If you are a deacon in Christ's church, these qualities should not have been merely an entrance exam to the office. Rather, each of these character traits should be yours and increasing. This passage describes the character of a deacon who serves well in the office. To this passage of Scripture, we now turn our attention in hopes that we might see how the character of a deacon is so closely related to the purpose of a deacon.

> Deacons, likewise, should be worthy of respect, not hypocritical, not drinking a lot of wine, not greedy for money, holding the mystery of the faith with a clear conscience. And they must also be

> tested first; if they prove blameless, then they can serve as deacons. Wives, too, must be worthy of respect, not slanderers, self-controlled, faithful in everything. Deacons must be husbands of one wife, managing their children and their own households competently. For those who have served well as deacons acquire a good standing for themselves, and great boldness in the faith that is in Christ Jesus. (1 Timothy 3:8–13)

This passage is often consulted when a church is considering new candidates for the diaconate. Rightly so. Certainly, these qualities should be evident long before a name is mentioned as a candidate. If you need a position or a title to selflessly do the work of a deacon, you're not qualified.

In this final chapter, let's examine the various components of this passage.

Reputation (v. 8)

John Maxwell's seventh "irrefutable law of leadership" is the "law of respect." "When leaders are respected and they ask for commitment, their people step up and sign up," he writes. "When respected leaders ask for change, followers willingly embrace it. But when leaders who are not respected ask for commitment or change, people doubt, they question, they make excuses, or they simply walk away. It is very hard for a leader who hasn't earned respect to get other people to follow."[33] Deacons must be "worthy of respect." Church and community members think of them as wise, trustworthy people. Church members will not follow leaders they believe are untrustworthy. For this reason, deacons should have a good rapport in the community and the church body.

It is noteworthy that the grammar of the original text accents the quality of the person ("*worthy of* respect") rather than the disposition of others toward him ("respected"). The emphasis is not on whether someone is respected, but on the individual's quality of respectableness. The question for a deacon or deacon candidate is not, "Is this person respected," but rather, "Is this person respectable?" Does the deacon *deserve* the respect given? Deacons are not to be called and ordained simply because they are respected. Only those whose character in Christ is *worthy* of respect should be considered.

The church's reputation in the community is often directly connected to its deacons' reputation in the community. I received a phone call one Tuesday afternoon from the city manager in a town where I was pastoring for a short season. He began, "Dr. Wolfe, one of your deacons just…" and he recounted an awful tale of how this man cheated, lied, and disparaged the city manager on a certain job. Then he preceded to tell me how the church had a negative reputation in the community because of things like this. I let him air it out, then asked for the deacon's name. When the name came across the phone, I sighed with relief. This person was not a deacon in the church. In fact, he was not even an active member. But the point was well taken that everywhere they go, perceived leaders in the church carry with them the power to build up or tear down the reputation of the congregation.

Deacons must be above reproach. Peter instructed Christian readers dispersed throughout a godless culture to testify to Christ with "gentleness and respect, keeping a clear conscience, so that when you are accused, those who disparage your good conduct will be put to shame," (1 Peter 3:16). If the deacon is to lead by example, his Christlike character must be evident both inside and outside the church body.

Sincerity (v. 8)

The Christian Standard Bible translates it "not hypocritical." The word is *dialogos*, literally, "double tongued." That's what hypocrites do. They say one thing but mean another. They have two standards in their words and actions: one standard for themselves and a different standard for others. Convenience and context decide what is right or wrong, according to what benefits them most in the moment. Having two standards allows them to always appear upright by their own measurement and to own the power of judgment toward others by a different measurement. Hypocrites. The most frequent answer I get when asking an unchurched person why he or she does not attend church is, "The church is full of hypocrites." On some level, this statement is true. None of us perfectly lives up to the Christian standards we confess, teach, and preach. But when the deacon fails in Christlike character, he admits it, apologizes, and grows from it. A deacon's sincerity stands in stark contrast to casual Christian hypocrisy.

The Lord was working powerfully in the small town where I pastored. I began meeting with a young man who had been transplanted there for work with the power company as a lineman. He repented from sin and placed his faith Jesus Christ, and I baptized him the next Sunday. Then I discipled him for several months. Only a few weeks into our discipleship journey, he called me in tears one stormy afternoon. He was working on a line outside the gas station owned by one of my deacons. Electricity had been out for hours because of the powerful storm that was passing through. He and the other linemen were doing the best they could. My deacon, not seeing the face of the man, stepped outside in the rain and cussed him up and down the power pole. The new Christian stepped inside his truck and called me immediately. He was crying, obviously distraught. He had previously looked up to this deacon as a model for faith and faithfulness in Christ. He told me what happened then said, "If that's what being a Christian is like, I don't want any part of it."

I gave him some quick counsel and calmed him down. When we hung up, I immediately called the deacon and told him about the conversation. Without saying a word, he hung up on me. Worried, I let it sit for a while and eventually he called me back. When he hung up on me, he stepped outside in the pouring rain, knocked on the window of this young man's work truck, and wept uncontrollably while asking for forgiveness. The new Christian told me about the whole episode when we talked about it later. On the deacon's return call to me he said, "Pastor, I need to resign as a deacon. I've failed Jesus, I've failed my church, and I've failed you." I responded, "No, sir. This young man does not need to get the idea that mature Christians are perfect. Rather, he needs to see that when they fail and sin, they own up to it, repent, and restore. That's what you've done." I prayed with the deacon over the phone and in the next week's discipleship meeting, I was pleased to learn that he and the young man had talked several times since that stormy night. In the following months, they became close friends and the young Christian's mentorship passed from me to this deacon who continued to pour his life into the growing Christ follower.

In all four purposes of the deacon position—lead, serve, support, and protect—sincerity is vital. If there is obvious hypocrisy in the deacon body, if there is any kind of double standard, then all four biblical purposes will be undermined. You cannot lead by example without sincerity. You cannot serve the membership without sincerity. You cannot support the pastor and church staff without sincerity. You cannot protect the peace without sincerity. The degree of a deacon's sincerity will directly correlate to the degree of his effectiveness in ministry.

Sobriety (v. 8)

"Not drinking a lot of wine" is the biblical standard of a deacon's consumption habits. The deacon is not to be a drunkard. Not addicted. Literally, "Not given to much wine." Most frequently in the New Testament, the same words are translated in warning language such as "beware," or "take heed." Scripture is replete with such warnings about alcohol consumption. Perhaps Proverbs 20:1 is most familiar: "Wine is a mocker, beer is a brawler; whoever goes astray because of them is not wise." A plethora of Old Testament scriptures portray alcohol and its consumption as corrupt and a corrupting agent (Proverbs 23:21; Isaiah 5:11, 19:14; Joel 1:5; Habakkuk 2:15; Hosea 4:11). Ephesians 5:18 juxtaposes the worthy pursuit of being filled with the Spirit against the debauchery of being drunk with wine. Galatians 5:19–21 lists drunkenness alongside sexual immorality, idolatry, outbursts of anger, "and anything similar" as a "work of the flesh." Paul writes, "I am warning you about these things."

Other biblical passages mention wine or strong drink in a positive connotation (Numbers 18:12; Psalm 104:14–15; Matthew 9:17; John 2:10–11; 1 Timothy 5:23). Here, space and purpose do not warrant or permit the detailing of a biblical theology of alcohol consumption. However, what is clear in 1 Timothy 3:3 and 3:8, among other passages, is that the Bible offers a clear warning about consumption for those who hold biblical offices. If deacons consume alcohol, in no way should they be mentally or socially affected by it. Nor should they be addicted to it. Far be it from me to legalistically forbid anything the Scriptures do not explicitly restrict. At the same time, a responsible biblical hermeneutic requires the strongest of warnings when it comes to the exercise of Christian liberty in this area.

In *Lead Like Jesus*, Ken Blanchard and Philip Hodges offer a careful word on the nature of addiction to any self-medicating substance or activity. "Addictions, both positive and negative, start as a voluntary attempt or choice to experience something desirable and end up as a compulsion that grows continually stronger and out of control. When we seek safety from pain and loss of self-esteem in at-risk things ... we are vulnerable to anxiety and fear as key drivers for our thoughts and behaviors."[34] Whether on emotional lows or adrenaline highs, all of us tend to self-medicate instead of finding our solace in Christ alone, by his Spirit alone. What is clear from the text of Scripture is that alcohol consumption is one of those "at-risk" behaviors that, if not properly subjected under the authority of Christ, can rob a person of joy and inhibit his or her ability to think clearly and act appropriately when under the influence, or even when desiring the substance.

Personally, I choose not to consume alcohol at all. I just don't need it, and exercising that freedom in Christ is something I am ready and willing to give up if it in any way might cause a stumbling block to others around me. However, I readily admit this is my personal conviction, not a biblical mandate. Some churches' deacon policies require complete abstinence to hold the office. Others allow for careful moderation. Either way, sobriety is the standard. At all times, whether in public or private, the deacon should be in complete control of his mental faculty, "full of the Spirit and wisdom" (Acts 6:3).

Generosity (v. 8)

In the contemporary western world, we have fallen into the trap of believing that more is better. As Richard Foster writes in *Celebration of Discipline*, "The modern hero is the poor boy who purposefully becomes rich rather than the rich boy who voluntarily becomes poor." In our "consumer society," he continues, "covetousness we call ambition. Hoarding we call prudence. Greed we call industry."[35]

It's amazing how, no matter where you keep it, your pocketbook is always in such close proximity to your heart. The deacon cannot be "greedy for money," writes the apostle Paul. Greed is a foul motivator for anything. But generosity is greed's archenemy. There is something special about generosity when it comes to giving to God's kingdom work through the church; it creates within you a singular devotion to the Great Commission.

Perhaps one of the most misunderstood verses of the Bible is a quick one-liner in the middle of Jesus's Sermon on the Mount: "For where your treasure is, there your heart will be also" (Matthew 6:21). I often hear a Bible teacher or preacher interpret this verse as if it suggests that when you love something enough, you invest in it—you invest in what you love. But Jesus's point is exactly the opposite. The more you invest in something, the more you come to love it—you love what you invest in. You know this to be true from your own experiences. The more time, money, and energy you put into a relationship, a hobby, a job, or an organization, the more you can't imagine your life without it. The more you invest in something, the more committed you are to it. We become beholden to that in which we sacrificially invest.

Imagine, deacon, sacrificially investing in the long-term health of your local church and in the glory of Christ through the advancement of the gospel to the ends of the earth. Imagine, over many decades, pouring your time, resources, energy, and affections into the good work that God is doing in and through your church. The more you invest, and the longer you invest, the more intensely you will come to love. This is Jesus's point. "Where your treasure is, there your heart will be also."

What are you investing in? Generous investments in God's kingdom yield an eternal harvest. Keep this in mind when it comes to greed and generosity: unsown fields yield mostly weeds. Perhaps a close look at the crops you are producing, as a deacon or a deacon body, will bear witness to the kind and measure of sowing you've been doing. The deacon cannot lead by example, serve the membership, support the staff, or protect the peace when his heart is calloused from greed. He must be a generous giver.

Conviction (v. 9)

In every generation, "holding the mystery of the faith with a clear conscience" is a non-negotiable character trait for the deacon on purpose. Christians who are infantile in their faith today will be confronted by many questions about the reliability of God's Word, the historicity of biblical claims, and the validity of their personal spiritual experiences. As the twenty-first century progresses, radically expressive individualism is usurping both timeless truth (modernism) and cause-oriented social constructivism (postmodernism) as the ultimate standard of reality. "The modern self assumes the authority of inner feelings and sees authenticity as defined by the ability to give social expression to the same," writes Carl R. Trueman in his 2022 book, *Strange New World*. This pattern of "expressive individualism," he explains, "is the normative way of thinking."[36] Now more than ever, the nature of biblical truth and its authority in the life of individuals is being called into question. Deacons must be secure in their biblical faith, "watching out" for themselves, so that the same temptation to deny or manipulate biblical truth will not befall them (Galatians 6:1).

We have an enemy who is cunning and persistent. He is the father of lies and the deceiver of the brethren (John 8:44). He is the ruler of the power of the air, roaming around like a lion seeking unsuspecting and weak prey to devour (Ephesians 2:2, 1 Peter 5:8). When Christians are appointed to an office in the church, he colors a bright red target on their back, draws back his bow, and looses his fiery darts with merciless precision. If the shield of faith cannot be wielded, injury and embarrassment will follow.

When we come to Christ and are being nurtured/discipled by more spiritually mature believers, the innocence and wonder of the Christian faith will enthrall our hearts and fill our minds. This is beautifully innocent and powerfully captivating. Like the Gerasene demoniac, the sponginess of new faith in Christ longs to sit and soak in his presence, but the Lord compels us to go and grow in our witness (Mark 5:18–19). It is an embarrassment to Christ and his church for those who should be mature in the faith to linger as infants (1 Corinthians 3:1–3). Maturing Christian faith is an exercise of both mind *and* heart, knowledge *and* will, faith *and* action. To acknowledge Christian truth is one thing. To "hold" it and live it is another. The one who knows the mystery of the faith without holding the mystery of the faith is a seedling in a tornado. But the one who holds that mystery "with a clear conscience" is an oak, immovable and secure even as the strongest winds press against his well-formed branches.

Deacon, I promise you this: many will question and oppose your faith. In some instances, their arguments will seem convincing. You don't have to answer all their objections, and no one expects you to be a professional Christian apologist. But you must be firm enough in your Christian faith to hold to it when it is challenged in new ways. And it will be.

Examination (v. 10)

"The path does not produce the change; it only places us where the change can occur." With timeless sagacity, Richard Foster shuffles the dirt along the trail of ancient wisdom: "This is the path of disciplined grace … once we live and walk on the path of disciplined grace for a season, we will discover internal changes."[37] Time itself does not guarantee spiritual maturity, but spiritual maturity requires a period of time. Regretfully, twenty-first-century evangelical churches are full of men and women who have walked with Jesus for decades but are not more spiritually mature today than they were then. They should be leading and teaching but instead they're still sitting and soaking.

Increasing spiritual maturity is a requirement for those who hold biblical offices. In my 2016 book *Mile Markers*, I propose three stages of spiritual growth from 1 John 2:12–14: spiritual infancy, spiritual adolescence, and spiritual adulthood. One of the most important markers of spiritual maturity is one's increasing awareness of growth still needed. To be mature and maturing is not to have arrived, but to have walked the road of Christian faithfulness for a season and to have been strengthened in the faith accordingly. Many who are approached to consider the office of deacon consider themselves unworthy, unknowledgeable, or unprepared. In essence, they feel they are not spiritually mature enough. This is a normal feeling for those who understand the importance of the office.

But deacon candidates must recognize that the work of Christian maturity is never completed this side of the grave. The 1 Timothy 3:10 character measurement is one of testing and proving, not testing and perfecting. "The more we know about God's Word the more we realize we do not know about God's Word. The more we come to know God through His Word, the more we long to know Him. The more Christlike we become, the more we realize how far we are from Christlikeness."

Knowledge, growth, and humility are all marks of maturity. But perhaps the most obvious marker of spiritual adulthood is intentional reproduction. Mature things reproduce. "A spiritual adult has a vested interest in the spiritual health of those he influences. And though he knows he is not perfect, he lives his life as an open model for Christian discipleship."[38]

It is wise for a deacon candidate to go through a season of testing/examination before being considered for the office. But remember, this is as much about character as it is about requirement. The time period itself is not the issue; the goal is to have clearly demonstrated spiritual maturity. James reminds his reader, "the testing of your faith produces endurance" (James 1:3). Testing for testing's sake is pointless. But testing for the sake of perseverance and endurance is biblical. Testing takes time. Don't appoint someone to the office hastily.

This may sound cold and reproving, but it needs to be said. I pray you receive it in love and grace, as it is intended. If you are having trouble finding qualified, capable deacon candidates in your church, the first person to blame is probably yourself. Many Christian leaders assume that *someone else* is evangelizing, discipling, and raising up leaders for the next generation of church offices. But they are not evangelizing, discipling, and raising up such leaders themselves. You know your congregation will need faithful, qualified deacons in the decades ahead.

In the Fall 2023 edition of *Deacon Magazine*, I unfolded a

practical, seven-fold strategy for "Selecting and Training Effective Deacons." Here are the seven steps:

(1) Pray.
(2) Build and facilitate clear discipleship pathways in the church.
(3) Evangelize in your community.
(4) Identify and begin discipling potential servant-leaders.
(5) Create a culture of mentorship in the deacon body.
(6) Develop a biblically and practically robust deacon training program.
(7) Make deacon selection and ordination special, prayerful ceremonies.[39]

Whatever system or strategy you adopt or build for your church, understand that one day you will be searching for qualified, faithful deacon candidates. Each of them must have endured a season of testing and examination. If you do not begin evangelizing, discipling, and mentoring potential candidates now, they will not be ready when the church needs them.

Imagine a deacon body full of men who have been examined over time and have been proven faithful. Imagine a group of deacons charged with the leadership, service, support, and protection of the church body who have steadfast endurance, no matter what kinds of trials come their way. This is the kind of deacon body the church needs, Paul tells Timothy. Examined. Tested. Disciplined. Secure.

Home Life (vs. 11–12)

The phrase "husband of one wife" tends to get most of the attention in verse 12. Whatever your church's position on this phrase, please don't forget that this phrase is about character. The deacon must be a one-woman kind of man. He must only have eyes for his one bride; he must be wholly devoted to his one wife.

As noted toward the beginning of this chapter, I believe

the most straight-forward reading of the biblical texts supports an all-male diaconate. However, I want to reiterate that many theologically conservative, biblically faithful pastors and church leaders believe differently on this matter and allow godly, faithful women to hold the office of deacon. I celebrate their commitment to the authority of Scripture and honor their autonomy in this decision. I personally know women who hold the office of deacon and will be the first to testify to their godliness, graciousness, humility, and faithfulness to Christ, his Word, and his church. This is not a first- or second-tier doctrinal matter, and it is not worth division or disunion between churches or within churches. I have also personally watched countless godly, faithful women graciously take up the responsibility of servant leadership in local churches without the title or office. Their willingness to serve edified and strengthened the church, and in some cases rescued the church from imminent demise. Whether or not godly, faithful women are allowed to hold the office and claim the title, they are by function deaconesses (female servants) of the church, worthy of our deepest respect and sincerest gratitude.

If a deacon is married, he must be faithful to his one wife. He must be a one-woman kind of man. According to verse eleven, his wife "also must be worthy of respect," not a slanderer or gossiper, "self-controlled, faithful in everything." Whether women hold the office and claim the title or not, if a deacon is married his wife must exhibit godliness, humility, and faithfulness in her character. Deacons who are married will often deacon, functionally, as a husband-and-wife team. They will make visits together, serve families together, and give their lives to the church together. Verse eleven cannot be overlooked when it comes to the deacon's home life. Too many office holders have become disqualified on account of their spouses' failures in the character qualities listed here. Most likely, you can recount as many first-hand stories as I can that demonstrate this truth.

Similarly, the deacon must be a faithful and wise leader in his home, "managing their own households and their own children competently," (verse 12). If the deacon has children, it should be evident in their lives that they have been encouraged toward righteousness, led toward Jesus, and intentionally discipled in the home. Eventually, all our children will make their own decisions and walk their own paths. But regardless the choices children make later in life, the deacon's home must be one in which Jesus was consistently honored as Lord. Smethurst simplifies, "The apostle could not be clearer: there is no such thing as a good deacon who is a lousy husband or dad. Being a 'good family man' is not a bonus in considering someone for the diaconate; it is a prerequisite."[40] The deacon's home must be a place of love, grace, forgiveness, discipleship, and hospitality. His wife and children will not be perfect, nor should they be held to that standard. However, he must have managed the affairs of his household well if he is to lead, serve, support, and protect the affairs of God's household. "He is being asked to serve the household of God. If his personal household is out of order, he will not be able to serve the church as he should."[41]

Reward (v. 13)

Verse 13 answers a question no deacon will ever ask. So allow me to ask it for you: What's in it for me? The very thought of this question likely offends those who are called to this office. They are, by nature, servants who seek no reward. Nonetheless, to those who serve well a reward is given. As an object itself, the reward is not to be sought, but it is also not to be despised. God gives good gifts to the children he loves (Matthew 7:11). You, deacon, are no exception. But this reward is not simply for those who have held the office or worn the title. It is exclusive to some within the deacon body. By logical extension, it is withheld from others. A literal translation of 1 Timothy 3:13 would employ the verb tense of the word "deacon," just as we saw in Acts 6:3—those who *deacon* well.

When the reward is considered, the question will not be "have you *deaconed?*" but "have you *deaconed* well?"

The Bible does not offer objective measurements of success for the deacon. There are no checkboxes for goal completion or change affected. The only expressed goal is to deacon well. Give it all you've got, all the time. Maybe that's a good thing. Very few know this about me (until now, when you all read this book), but I am legitimately obsessive-compulsive. I've dealt with it my whole life. It often works itself out in the strangest and most subtle ways. I won't bore you with the details. Suffice it to say that I often subconsciously default to living my life by checking boxes. I set small goals for myself (often daily), write them down, and literally check or scratch them off. That may sound strange to you, but it's just part of who I am. It helps me manage anxiety and live above some of my self-inflicted psychological wounds. Sometimes I tell people I have CDO. It's like OCD, except in alphabetical order. I know, I'm odd. You'll never look at me the same.

If I were called to be a deacon and Scripture listed clear, objective measurements of success, I am confident that I would enslave myself to them daily. I have no doubt about this; it's just part of who I am. But as we have explored throughout this book, a deacon is not a robot. A deacon is a spiritually vibrant, relationally engaged, Spirit-led servant-leader. That is not to say deacons cannot or should not be organized and systematic. Quite the opposite! But at the end of the day, measurements of success will never be quantified by the boxes you check. In many ways, the reward of deaconing is baked into the bread of daily rhythms. Serve well, and you will know exactly what I'm talking about.

According to verse 13, the reward of a deacon who has "served well" is two-fold: (1) "a good standing," and (2) "great boldness in the faith." A good standing in the church refers to the relational influence that develops over time as the deacon is found to be trustworthy. It is that measure of earned "respect" that "comes horizontally from the church."[42] After many years of serving well as a deacon on purpose, the church begins to see this man as someone they can trust and respect. This good standing is not a pin of honor fastened to the sportscoat for recognition in meetings. It's more like a pair of kneepads, hidden beneath the pant legs for greater comfort while washing feet. A deacon always stands tallest on his knees; he is most honorable when he is most humbled.

The second part of the faithful deacon's two-fold reward is that he acquires "great boldness in the faith." Faith is emboldened as godly men live a lifetime of service in the church. It's amazing how God uses every passing year to mold and shape us into the Christ followers he desires us to be. After decades of leading, serving, supporting, and protecting Christ's Bride, the deacon's faith becomes strong. He acquires "great boldness in the faith." What a blessing! What a reward!

Questions for Group Reflection/Discussion

1. What did you read in this chapter that challenged the way you have traditionally interpreted something inside the "qualification" passages for deacons? Do you agree or disagree, and why?

2. In your own words, how does this list of qualifications double as a list of character descriptions for the deacon?

3. Think back on the four purposes of the deacon (Lead by Example, Serve the Membership, Support the Pastor/Staff, Protect the Peace). How might a character failure in one or more of the areas listed in this chapter negatively affect the deacon's ability to serve well?

4. What is your church's understanding of 1 Timothy 3:8–12 regarding (a) divorce, (b) alcohol consumption, and (c) women holding the office? Talk through these issues as you study the Scriptures together and come to a consensus. If you disagree, do so lovingly and respectfully. You don't have to decide and make

changes today, but you'll never find consensus if you don't begin the conversation.

5. What are some practical ways your deacons can encourage and challenge one another regularly in these eight areas of character formation from 1 Timothy 3:8–13?

Afterword

My mom, now 74 years old, has always loved puzzles. When we were kids, she would buy a puzzle of 2,000 or 3,000 pieces and spread it out across the dining table where it would lay for weeks until she finally got it all together. My brothers and I would all sit with her at the table occasionally, searching for adjoining pieces and contributing to the project. Have you ever put together a puzzle with that many pieces? No matter how good you are, there is only one way to go about it. You can't put the pieces together unless you have a picture of the finished project in front of you. Every puzzle mom bought came packaged in a box with the finished picture printed on the front. While we worked on putting the puzzle together, we consulted the picture regularly. There were so many pieces. We could not have put them all together if we didn't have a picture of the finished product.

Deacons are the picture on the front of the puzzle box for everyday Christians. They do not always portray the finished product in perfection. Even close up, theirs is a downscaled and pixelated representation of Christian maturity. But that picture of faithfulness to Christ, family, and community is invaluable to church members. Life is so complex. Christians are trying to put together the pieces of their families, their jobs, their ministry involvement, their relationships, and so much more. Thankfully, God has given them a picture on the front of the box. He has gifted the church body with deacons as pictures of faithfulness to Christ, his church, and his world.

Traveling to train and encourage deacons over these last seven years has been one of the greatest joys of my life. I have been encouraged by countless faithful, godly deacons who are devoting the best of their lives to the cause of Christ in and through their local churches. Some are doctors and lawyers who trade in their lab coats and suits for towels and rags every time they enter the church gathering. Others are simple farmers and mechanics who have little more to offer than faithfulness to Christ and his people, and that has always proven more than enough. Still others are retired tradesmen, business owners, or schoolteachers whose character and relational influence over many years brings priceless gravity to every congregational decision. Over many state lines and across many waters, I have been enriched by the lives and testimonies of faithful deacons whose stories of selfless servitude to Christ's churches will not be told until heaven's ledger is opened.

The picture on the front of the box does not look the same in every local church context. I have witnessed a beautiful diversity in the representation of everyday faithfulness to Christ on display in a thousand deacons' faces within their local communities. Their churches are blessed by them, and I am too.

Occasionally, I will hear a pastor say something negative about deacons in general. I always respond by encouraging him to do the work of cultivating healthy relationships with those deacons, and to honor their biblical office the way he expects them to honor his. I have also encountered a few pastors who boast that they have "done away" with deacons altogether in their church. My heart breaks for them and for their congregations. Leading and serving the church alone may sound like a dream, but everywhere I have seen it, it's been a nightmare. God gave the church two offices. They are good, and they are interdependent. If the Bible presents two biblical offices for the New Testament church, as we so believe and confess, then training, encouraging, and purposing the deacon body is worth the effort. Most pastors continue to train their whole lives for the biblical office they hold. Why should deacons be any different?

I believe that when churches recapture the biblical design for the office of deacon, the Holy Spirit will work with refreshing power in and through them as a congregation. I believe Christ's people will have contextual pictures of everyday Christian living to look to while they grow up in the faith. I believe the church will begin to see more and more acts of selfless servitude as the people follow the example of their official servant leaders. I believe the membership will feel more connected and more loved than ever before. I believe the pastors and church staff will become more efficient in their time management and more encouraged in their own calling. I believe every conflict will be turned into opportunity as official servant leaders carefully, biblically, and graciously protect the peace and redirect problems toward growth in wisdom and power of the Holy Spirit. Why do I believe these things? Because that's what God did in Acts 6:1–7 and in countless churches since. When deacons lead well, serve well, love well, and relate well, churches thrive. It's not anecdotal. It's biblical.

I pray you have discovered new energy and received timely refreshment in your calling through the course of this book. And I pray that new energy is directed prayerfully and practically toward serving your church with a renewed sense of passion and determination. Your call is sure, and your time is short. God has ordained. You have answered. The church has approved. Your pastors have prayed. You are not a deacon on accident, so be a deacon on purpose.

Appendix

The following 17 articles were published in
Lifeway's Deacon Magazine between 2019–2023.
They offer biblical insights and practical suggestions on specific topics
related to deacon ministry in and through the local church.

"10 Practical Ways to Encourage Your Pastor"

Every pastor needs encouragement. The weight of the job is intense enough on its own, keeping watch over your souls as one who will give an account to God (Hebrews 13:17). When the weight of the pastoral office is compounded by conflicting personalities, community crisis, major decisions, and critical church members, the pastor's spirit can sometimes break beneath the pressure. No pastor can perform at his best with a broken spirit: "A person's spirit can endure sickness, but who can survive a broken spirit?" (Pr. 18:14)

Most pastors are their own worst critics. Some have plenty of external sources of discouragement around them to claim that title. How do you, as a deacon, become proactive about mending and maintaining the spirit of your pastor? In a word—encouragement. Intentional, regular, relentless encouragement. Encouraged pastors pray better, lead better, preach better, and shepherd better. Here are ten simple yet significant ways you can encourage your pastor today.

1. **Pray with him**. Set up an appointment to stop by his office and just pray with him. Pray for his personal life, his family, his leadership decisions, his influence in the community, and everything else you can think of. When you regularly pray with and for your pastor, over time your hearts become knit together in life and in ministry. It's one thing to say, "I'm praying for you, pastor." It's something else entirely to schedule time out of your day to pray with and over him.

2. **Send him an encouraging text**. It does not need to be long. A simple, "I just wanted you to know right now that I appreciate you, pastor," can cut through the discouragement of a tense moment. It can brighten the whole day or lift the spirit at just the right time. I am often amazed at how God puts this simple, practical ministry opportunity on my heart and into my thumbs at just the right moment for someone. When the Holy Spirit puts him on your heart, shoot him a text and let him know you're thinking about him and you love him.

3. **Mail him a handwritten card**. There is something simple yet powerful about a handwritten card of appreciation or encouragement. Your pastor gets lots of things in his mailbox: bills he can't pay, advertisements for things he can't afford, letters of complaint he can't avoid, and much more. Be the deacon to make his day at the mailbox by simply putting a handwritten card or note of encouragement in the mail.

4. **Take him to breakfast or lunch**. Not to complain or to get something out of him. Just to build friendship and let him know you care about him. Force the conversation to revolve only around him and his family, his hobbies, or his academic pursuits. Find out what day and time works best for him and take him to his favorite restaurant, or to yours. The early church learned, "from house to house," that there is something surprisingly supernatural about sharing a meal in gratitude to God and in fellowship with one another. With only a few dollars from your wallet and an hour

from your calendar, you can know this joy as well.

5. **Give him a gift for no reason.** What commentary or book has he been wanting? What does he collect? What activities does he enjoy? A simple gift given for no particular reason and with no strings-attached is a great way to say, "I appreciate you, and I'm for you."

6. **Champion him on social media.** When we speak of "public praise, private correction," most critics lean toward the latter and tend to forget the former. Your pastor receives plenty of private correction (and public correction, too). Choose to be the deacon who champions him publicly. Don't patronize him and don't overdo it. But every now and then, just give him a simple shout-out on social media so the whole world can see that you love and appreciate your pastor.

7. **Bless his family.** As a pastor myself, there were very few things a deacon could do that encouraged me more than taking the time and energy to bless my family. My deacons made being a pastor's kid something special when they took my boys hunting or fishing, wrote them cards, and invested in them personally. Few things discourage a pastor more than when his family is dispirited or ignored. You can infuse hope and joy into your pastor's life and ministry by doing simple things to bless his wife and children.

8. **Organize a pastor appreciation gift or event.** October is Pastor Appreciation Month every year. But many churches let it pass without any recognition at all. Don't be that church. Begin now to organize small groups, church leaders or those creative and hospitable people in your church family to make Pastor Appreciation Month special this year. Honor him with a tangible gift, a monetary blessing, a plaque in recognition, or a special day of fellowship and appreciation.

9. **Defend him publicly.** Refuse to get pulled into the weeds in ridiculous accusations. But at the same time, take up for your pastor's honor and integrity when it is called into question. Even if you disagree with his decisions, you can stand up for his character.

The Apostle Paul lamented that when accusations came his way, no one stood with him (2 Timothy 4:16). No Christian minister should ever have to stand for truth alone. When the opportunity presents itself, under the guiding humility of the Holy Spirit, stand with your pastor and stand for your pastor.

10. **Ask him what you can take off of his plate.** Deacons serve as an extension of the pastor's long arm of ministry. One of the best ways you can encourage your pastor is to ask what you can take off of his plate this week. Is there a visit you can make for him? A menial task you can perform for him? A meeting you can handle in his place? When deacons lighten the pastor's ministerial load, they encourage him greatly.

Deacon, you and your pastor are on the same team. Teams function at their best when their interaction is infused with the language and actions of encouragement. Take the initiative today to be a regular, intentional encourager for your pastor. The return on such an investment can only be calculated in terms of eternity.

"Back to the Basics: What it Means to be a Baptist Deacon"

"When we completed our voyage from Tyre, we reached Ptolemais, where we greeted the brothers and sisters and stayed with them for a day. The next day we left and come to Caesarea, where we entered the house of Philip the evangelist, who was one of the Seven, and stayed with him. This man had four virgin daughters who prophesied. After we had been there several days … ." (Acts 21:7–10)

I am writing in early 2022. Is it just me or have the last two years felt like ten? Worldwide pandemic, denominational conflict, racial unrest, economic instability, revivals of terrorism, new definitions of sex and sexuality, political upheaval, technological breakthrough. If the church is trying to keep up or catch up, I'm afraid it's already too late. But maybe that's not altogether bad. Has the church's ambition ever really been to keep up or catch up with changing cultural winds?

Certainly, we are to be students of our time. God has called us to this moment rather than to any other. But it is true in our day, as it has been in every other day, that the new thing God is doing is really a very old thing. The mission of God has not changed. He is still redeeming men and women who will come to him in repentance from sin and faith in Jesus Christ. He is still making disciples of all nations. And he has called us to this timeless mission in our contemporary world.

Maybe what we need is not a new strategy or a new plan. Maybe what we need is to get back to the basics. If deacons are going to serve the church well in this new age, then it will be by holding to the same basic New Testament pattern that is laid for our faith and practice. Deacons in every age will serve well when they anchor their ministry in the timeless, basic principles of their biblical prototypes.

When I coached my sons in basketball, most of our time was invested in rehearsing fundamentals. Sure, we ran plays in practice and rehearsed offensive and defensive drills. But most of the work, both on and off the court, majored in rehearsing fundamentals. If the fundamentals were great, any game-play scenario could be navigated with skill.

I am convinced that if a deacon will get great at the fundamentals, he will be able to navigate any game-play scenario with excellence. So, let's get back to basics. Look with me on Deacon Philip of Caesarea, one of our New Testament prototypes, and see four fundamentals of being a great deacon in any generation.

1. **Be a servant.** Philip was a servant. It was his default mode. When Paul and his missionary company needed a place to rest

after months of strenuous, demanding ministry, they knew right where to go. Deacon Philip, one of the Seven from Acts 6:1–7, opened his home and served them for several days. I imagine Philip preparing their meals, washing their clothes, and providing for a variety of other simple, everyday needs. It wasn't a glamorous ministry. But it was a necessary one. When the pastors and missionaries needed to be served, Philip defaulted to servant mode, because that's just who he was.

In 2022 and beyond, deacons need to get back to simply being a servant. Serve the church. Serve the pastors. Serve the community. Serve the denomination. Just serve people. It's basic, I know. But it's what we do.

2. **Share the gospel.** Philip was an evangelist. In Acts 8, under the influence of the Holy Spirit, Philip led the Ethiopian eunuch to faith in Jesus Christ. Apparently, this was only one of Philip's many notable evangelistic encounters because twenty-eight years later the descriptor stuck. In Acts 21:8, Luke called him, "Philip the evangelist." You may or may not have the positional calling of an Ephesians 4:11 evangelist, but you do have the commission of an Acts 1:8 evangelistic witness.

With the dawn of every new cultural day, deacons need to be about the basic business of bearing witness to Jesus Christ. They need to share the gospel with lost people and invite them to respond in repentance and faith. There is no evangelistic church growth without evangelistic witness. And there is no evangelistic witness without witnesses who evangelize. It's a fundamental thing. A simple, thing, really. Regardless the cultural season, deacons should be evangelizing the lost.

3. **Lead your homes well.** Philip led his home well. Acts 21:9 tells us he had four virgin daughters who prophesied. Why include that piece of information? I'm sure there could be any number of reasons. But one that cannot be overlooked is that Philip was not merely a man who was himself devoted to God. He led his

home in such a way that his family would also devote themselves to God. Philip discipled in his home. He taught his daughters to know and proclaim God's Word.

Deacons in our contemporary culture need to model biblical discipleship in their homes. Perhaps one of the most disturbing contemporary trends is the continued breakdown of the biblical home structure. It should be such a basic thing. It's a Christian fundamental. To lead well in the church and in the community, you must start in your own home. Our generation needs deacons who lead their homes with distinction in discipleship, worship, evangelism, hospitality, and other simple daily rhythms of grace.

4. **Embrace faithful longevity.** Philip was faithful. In Acts 8, Paul was the persecutor and Philip the evangelist. In Acts 21, twenty-eight years later, Paul was the missionary and Philip was still the evangelist. Much had changed in twenty-eight years, but the deacon's role and passions remained the same. Philip was steady and consistent in his faith and in his ministry to the church through the years.

Oh, how we need deacons today who are faithful and consistent in their ministry to the church. We need real-time models of what Eugene Peterson called *A Long Obedience in the Same Direction.* Will you be that deacon? The culture around you is changing at a whiplashing pace. It's full of real people who have real problems to which there is but one real solution. They need Christ. And they need to encounter Christ through the lives and voices of faithful servants who have remained steadfast in their commitment to him through the years. In a world where change seems the only constant, faithfulness in life and ministry is an attractive rarity. Live the difference. Be steady. Be faithful.

Neither of my sons ended up playing basketball in college or as a career. But they both learned some valuable, timeless lessons from it. Perhaps one of the greatest lessons they learned was that fundamentals matter. When you focus on excellence in the basic rhythms of a craft, getting the win in real-time scenarios comes as the natural overflow. Fundamentals fuel instinct. Today and in every day, the church needs deacons with New Testament instincts.

The truth is, I don't know what 2022 or 2023 or 2030 are going to bring. I imagine in our culture, at the current pace of change, tomorrow will look very different from today. But here's what I know. Those deacons who serve with distinction through it all will be those who have excelled in the fundamentals of their calling. The fundamental rhythms of being a biblical deacon will give them everything they need in every passing moment to serve the church and honor Christ with excellence. Be that deacon. Major on the fundamentals. Get back to the basics.

"Building a Lasting Legacy: Passing on Faith to the Next Generation"

"Even while I am old and gray, God, do not abandon me, while I proclaim your power to another generation, your strength to all who are to come." (Psalm 71:18)

"We work on our annual audit every day." An odd sentence to open a deacon article, I know. But it has everything to do with leaving a legacy of faith for generations of Christ followers to come. Joe was the CFO of the Baptist non-profit missions organization for which I worked. He was also a faithful deacon in his church. January through February every year, I saw him and his team meeting occasionally with our external auditors to verify our financial records. I cannot remember a single time under his leadership that an audit came back without the highest marks. One day we were talking about how much time it really takes for his team to work on the audit every year. He replied, "We work on our annual audit every day." Every penny. Every entry. Every detail. Every day. Joe leads his team in everyday excellence and everyday accountability, with the annual audit in mind. So, when January comes around, the work is already mostly done.

When I lead deacon trainings, my favorite discussion question to ask comes at the end of the first session. I prompt attendees to share about deacons from their past who have influenced them positively in their walk with Jesus and in their service to his church. Once this discussion gets started, it is difficult to stop. Everyone in the room recalls at least one deacon from their past who modeled sacrificial servitude, faithful witness, biblical wisdom, relational intentionality, spiritual vibrancy, or any number of other notable traits for an influential Christ follower. Some acknowledge that this deacon directly or indirectly inspired them to be ready to hold the office when the church called on them to do so. Influence is a stewardship, and for the deacon it is a stewardship that must be realized with generations in mind.

How do you quantify a deacon's legacy? What character traits, acts of service, or moments in time should constitute that corpus of faith and faithfulness by which a deacon who has "served well" (1 Timothy 3:13) should be remembered? I imagine such a list to be unique for each deacon. Stephen was eulogized as a deacon "full of grace and power" (Acts 6:8). Phillip will forever be known as the demon-exercising, gospel-preaching, personal-evangelist deacon with the gift of hospitality (Acts 8:4–40, 21:8). When your life is audited in the years ahead, what will future generations remember about you?

Like my friend Joe and his team, you are working on your legacy every day. Whether intentionally or unintentionally, every day you are making investments in, or withdrawals from, the legacy of faith and faithfulness you will leave behind. You are always influencing people. Every moment. Every decision. Every word. Every action. To leave a legacy worthy of your calling in Christ, you will need to live with the impending audit in mind.

When I think of Joe and his servant-heart at home, church and work, I can't help but recall the veracity and everyday excellence of the Lord Jesus. Jesus wasted no moment, no word, and no relationship. Every breath was an investment in his one purpose: his redemptive work on the cross and out of the grave. The work of Jesus was the work of God (John 5:19). Comparatively, every good work that Christ accomplishes through my friend Joe is a work of God's own power and strength. Joe knows this very well and is quick to give God all the glory, redirecting all praise Christward.

Beyond the personal traits for which you will be positively remembered, I pray one thing is true of you as it is true of Joe: that your legacy as a deacon is more about God than you. Ultimately, the legacy we leave as followers of Christ should not be a celebration of ourselves. Rather, as the Psalmist insists, the *power* and *strength* (Psalm 71:18) of the eternal God in Christ should be the essential content of every remembrance of our faith. A faith worth living is a faith worth reproducing when the great object of our faith, Jesus himself, is the focal point of the legacy we leave behind.

"Chess Not Checkers: Developing a Long-Term Strategy for Selecting and Training Effective Deacons"

To be transparent, I am not a great chess player. I usually do well to remember the difference between a bishop and a knight, and I often sneak in a quick Google search to be sure I'm putting the right piece on the right square. Still, I deeply appreciate the game. It's not like checkers. Sure, strategy is important in checkers, but it's not the same. The levels of complexity in the game of chess, with all the independent pieces and how they move, make more detailed, long-term strategy necessary to get the win, especially if you're up against a formidable foe.

In 2015, Mark Miller of Chick-Fil-A released his book *Chess Not Checkers*—a short, thought-provoking parable on leadership development in the context of business management. Miller argues for a long-game, strategic mindset when it comes to developing leaders in any organization. "If you play checkers when the name of the game is chess," he writes, "you lose."

The church of Jesus is up against a formidable foe. For thousands of years, Satan has been playing chess while many of us have been playing checkers. I cannot count the number of times I have heard a pastor or deacon chairman lament, "Tony, we desperately need more deacons, but we just don't have any qualified and capable candidates." Miller confronts this sentiment with timely, parabolic wisdom, "You can't wait until you need a leader to start developing one."

So, how does a church develop a long-term strategy for selecting and training effective deacons?

1. **Pray.** If your chess playing is anything like mine, prayer certainly couldn't hurt. However, we are not playing games with Jesus's church. Our Father's business is serious business. Have you been praying for God to raise up leaders in your church? When Jesus directed the eyes of his disciples to the white fields, he immediately instructed them to "pray that the Lord of the harvest will send workers into the fields." Leadership development in the church begins with prayer. It cannot begin anywhere else.

2. **Build and facilitate clear discipleship pathways in the church.** As gameplay in chess usually begins with the smallest pieces, long-term strategy for the development of church leaders begins in the preschool ministry. Work with your church leadership and with associational and denominational leaders to develop a discipleship pathway for all ages in your church that takes them through a gradual, systematic approach to Bible study and application. If you want spiritually mature adult church leaders in the trenches, you'll have to start

building them in the children's wing.

3. **Evangelize men in your community.** A chess match does not begin with the pieces magically appearing on the squares. Players must locate the pieces and position them on the board. It grieves me to hear a pastor say, "We just don't have any men in the church." Without reservation I always respond, "Go get some!" When's the last time you labored in prayer for a particular person, that God would save him through your gospel witness and then allow you the grace of discipling him, baptizing him, and helping him assimilate into the Body of Christ? Your church's future leaders are in your community. Go get them.

4. **Identify and begin discipling potential servant-leaders.** The best chess players are always thinking 5–10 moves ahead. An effective strategy includes multiple offensive and defensive fronts, several plays already in motion when others just begin. Ask God to show you five to ten men in the church whom he might call to a church office one day. Ask each of them, one by one, to commit to an intentional discipleship relationship with you for six months. Walk through a good theology book and discuss real-time church issues with them. Tell them you see the hand of God on their lives, and you believe in them. Repeat this with a new group annually and watch how God begins to strengthen the core of your church and raise up leaders.

5. **Create a culture of mentorship in the deacon body.** Chess is challenging and multifaceted; it takes time and repetition to learn how to play well. Those who have risen to the top, called "grandmasters," often take on apprentices to mentor and coach. In this way they reproduce skilled game players for generations to come. Intentional mentorship is the oldest education system in human history. Deacons should be reaching out to younger potential candidates and taking them along on visits, ministry projects, and evangelistic outings. Take another with you. Let him into your life. Show him the way.

6. **Develop a biblically and practically robust, perennial deacon training program.** Progressing in skill and wisdom does not come with frivolity, even in a game of wooden pieces. It takes decades of devoted study, practical repetition, and skill-sharpening. How much more time and energy should we invest in Christ's call to service his church? Take fifteen minutes at the beginning of deacon meetings to discuss a primary doctrine or to work through a chapter of a deacon training resource. Use the Baptist Faith and Message as a guide, or a theology book chosen by your pastor. Work through deacon training resources like *A Deacon On Purpose* or *The Deacon Ministry Handbook*. "As iron sharpens iron, so one man sharpens another." Stay sharp.

7. **Make deacon selection and ordination special, prayerful ceremonies.** Hundreds of thousands of fans do not fill stadiums every weekend to watch chess matches. But those who do attend respect and appreciate the game; they come expecting to think, to learn, to witness something remarkable, and to be drawn into the gravity of the moment. If you want to create a culture of respect for and devotion to the deacon office—a culture that celebrates and invites replication—then make selection and ordination services meaningful and participative. Invite church membership to take part in the ceremony through Scripture reading, guided prayer moments, responsive readings, and commitment statements. Do not idolize the deacon office, but do not trivialize it either.

As Miller's book concludes, he writes, "In chess, the more pieces you involve in the game, the greater your chances of winning." To develop a long-term strategy for selecting and training effective deacons, you'll need the buy-in of existing leaders and future candidates. The more possible candidates you assimilate into the pipeline, the more from which the congregation can choose when it's time. Start prayerfully. Start young. Start strategically. Start now.

"Deacons On Mission At Work"

To quote a friend of mine, "God never told lost people to go to church; he told the church to go to lost people." In Acts 1:8, Jesus gave Downtown Jerusalem Church her mission statement: to be his witnesses in Jerusalem, Judea, Samaria, and to the ends of the earth. But it took seven chapters for them to get moving from Jerusalem into Judea and Samaria. In fact, it took the martyrdom of a deacon, Stephen, to get the people of God moving with the mission. What will it take for the people of your local church to get moving with the mission?

The gospel of Jesus Christ should be advancing through your local church around the corner and across the globe. God has gifted the church with deacons to both serve the membership and set the example for them in faith and practice. Deacons are not to deacon only beneath a steeple, but in the community at large. Since 50 percent of your waking hours are spent at work every day, and since God has sent you to your coworkers to be his witness, the workplace is a mission field for every deacon. The work environment is a place to build relationships for kingdom purposes and faithfully share the gospel with those who are far from God. This is more than coincidence. It is God's design.

Here are five steps toward being on mission at work:

1. Work with a Colossians 3:17 ethic.

Christians who are lazy or unethical at work are bearing false witness to Christ. But those who work with diligence and skill make the name of Jesus great. In everything you do, whether pouring coffee or engineering bridges, transcribing courtroom recordings or composing orchestral masterpieces, do your work as if Jesus himself has asked you to do it and is standing over your shoulder. If your tongue speaks Christ's message while your hands idle with lazy indifference, you are sending mixed messages to your employer and fellow employees. Work hard, "as unto the Lord." The receptivity of the gospel you share can either be built upon or hindered by your work ethic. Make every second count.

2. **Work with a Philippians 2:5 mindset.**

   Paul writes, "Let the same attitude be in you that was in Christ Jesus. ... He humbled himself." In the corporate world, when someone climbs far enough up the ladder he or she is generally thought to be above certain things. But the deacon, following Christ's example, has willingly placed himself underneath everyone. If there is one defining character quality of a deacon it should be humility. Nothing is beneath a deacon's willingness to serve. Your witness for Christ cannot be divorced from your service to people. The deacon at work, on mission, remembers the value of every human being created in the image of God. Aloof pride is completely broken wherever Christlike humility is embraced. Work with the attitude of Christ, and watch how doors will open for the gospel.

3. **Work with a James 5:16 prayer radar.**

   If you are a new creation in Christ, God has imputed to you his righteousness. And while you are living from the overflow of God's grace you are actively doing righteous things. The deacon on mission is a righteous man not because of anything he has done, but because of all that Christ has done in him and is doing through him. This righteousness is both a blessing and a responsibility. James writes that such a man prays with powerful effect. As you humbly serve the people in your workplace with the attitude of Christ Jesus, listen for their concerns, fears, or needs and offer to pray with them. You may be surprised how willing people are for you to pray with them. Pray fervently for their concerns privately as well. When God answers prayers, celebrate it with them and point them to Jesus. A Christlike attitude in a hard worker opens doors to communicated concerns. Communicated concerns open doors to prayerful supplication. Answered prayers open doors to the gospel.

4. Work with an Acts 8:29–30 discernment.

The Holy Spirit told Deacon Philip where to go, and when he got there the Spirit showed him why. Philip happened upon a man studying the Scriptures and asked a non-condemning, simple question: "Do you understand what you are reading?" When a man is sensitive to the moving of the Holy Spirit, God reveals opportunities for spiritual conversations. Does anyone at your workplace bring his or her Bible? Do they have Scripture verses posted on their walls? Do you sense an openness to hearing and receiving God's Word? Consider starting a Bible study before work or during lunch. Keep it simple. Start with a six-week study or work through a short book of the Bible one chapter at a time. People are more likely to commit to short term opportunities than indefinite ones. Who at work is open to hearing the Word of God? Be discerning, like Deacon Philip. And facilitate opportunities for your coworkers to study Scripture together.

5. Work with a 2 Timothy 4:5 gospel readiness.

"Do the work of an evangelist," Paul instructs the young pastor. He does not bother asking if Timothy has the "gift of the evangelist." No, just do the work. How are the people in your workplace going to hear the gospel if you don't tell them? God made no mistake when he placed you in their circle of influence. You are exhibiting a biblical work ethic with a Christlike attitude, praying regularly for your coworkers and looking for gospel opportunities. But their eternity remains unchanged until you share the simple gospel message and invite them to respond. There's a lot going on at the workplace. I know. But while you do the temporal work, don't forget the eternal work. While you do *your* work, don't forget to do *the* work. Do the work of an evangelist. Be a deacon on mission at work.

"Deacons Standing Firm: Courage in the Face of Declining Church Attendance"

Summer is fun for families, but it can be hard on a church. Vacations, summer sports leagues, and irregular church activity schedules often make for an unpredictable season of attendance. This is especially true for those churches that are already noticing a downward trend in weekly attendance. Sometimes you can point to a certain event that began the decline. Perhaps it was a pastor's exit, a relational conflict, a community tragedy, a major change, a health crisis, or even an unpopular biblical stance on a timely issue. Other times, the stimulus is less determinable. In any scenario, it is challenging for church leadership to face seasons of declining attendance with courage and commitment. But that is exactly what we should do.

It is easy to be courageous when excitement is in the air. There is a rhythmic momentum to spiritual vitality when attendance is climbing, finances are promising, and baptism waters are stirring. The risk is low, and the reward is high. However, it is a different story altogether to be courageous through a noticeable slump. Sometimes you do all the right things, holding firm to the faith, but attendance steadily declines. Your biblical logic tells you that numbers don't matter, but there's something in your spirit that says they really do.

Chances are there is nothing a deacon can say or do immediately to reverse the trend. Usually, many factors are involved, and the pastor(s) of the church really needs to lead through the season with steady hands and a pure heart. Course correction takes time and endurance. How do you keep courageously moving forward when it feels like you're constantly swimming upstream? What does it look like to be a courageous deacon when church attendance is declining? Here are four suggestions:

1. **Show up.** An undeniable sociological dynamic is at play when fewer and fewer people are an active part of something, even when that something is weekly church attendance. It's the "sinking ship" phenomenon. But deacons lead by example. They don't jump ship. They show up to worship, give, serve, and grow, even if no one else does. In Luke 1:5–7, Zechariah and Elizabeth exhibited courageous faith in religiously showing up to the temple for decades even when their one prayer had not been answered. You know they were mocked. You know they were the gossip of the town. But all that mattered to Zechariah and Elizabeth was that they knew their presence at the temple was a matter of obedience to the Lord. They just kept showing up, and God rewarded their faithfulness more than they could have ever imagined.

2. **Trust Jesus.** Either this is Jesus's church, or it's not. Either he is building it, or he isn't. Either the word he sends out will accomplish what he intends, or it won't. You can choose what to believe about who Jesus is and what he said, but I have decided I'm just going to trust him. That's my entire game plan for life. What's yours? John 6 begins with a large crowd following Jesus. The next day, half as many looked for him across the sea. By the end of the chapter, there were only twelve, and one of them was soon to defect. Jesus grew his church from five thousand to eleven in a single chapter. By the standards of many today, it was a total failure. But you know better. What Jesus would accomplish through the fiery few in the next generation was more than a lukewarm crowd could ever have achieved. Why did the eleven remain? Because Jesus had the words of life. Where else would

they go? Jesus's teaching was hard. His methods were unusual. The crowds lost interest, but the faithful few remained. Why? Because they trusted Jesus. Shouldn't we?

3. **Support your pastor.** When attendance is declining, critics abound. Chances are, however, that your pastor is his own worst critic. He doesn't need your criticism. He needs your encouragement and support. It is a courageous thing to support your pastor when so many others are against him. To jump on their bandwagon, whether privately or publicly, is to contribute to their spiritual deprivation. But to support your pastor, in both truth and love, is to exhibit courageous commitment to Christ's superintending headship in the church. The Apostle Paul is arguably the most successful missionary of the church age. But his work for Christ was not without difficulty or disappointment. In a physically and spiritually distressful season, after thirty years of Christian ministry, Paul wrote to Timothy, "no one came to stand by me" (2 Tim 4:16). Let that sink in. No one came. No one was with him. Not one person. No one. I pray those words might never be uttered from your pastor's mouth. Support and encourage your pastor through seasons of declining attendance.

4. **Remember the mission.** Your mission is not to build the church. That's Jesus's work. Your mission is to make disciples. When a deacon expresses frustration over the direction of the church, I often ask how many times he has shared the gospel with someone that week. Then I'll ask how many new believers he is discipling right now. I'm sure you can imagine the responses. In Acts 6, there are too many church members to count. Seven deacons are installed to serve the widows. In Acts 7, Deacon Stephen preaches a compelling evangelistic sermon and is stoned to death for it. In Acts 8:1, the Jerusalem church declines from thousands worshipping in public to handfuls in dark corners fearing for their lives. But Deacon Phillip evangelized Samaria out in public. Then the Ethiopian eunuch. Even in the face of

persecution and congregational disruption, Phillip remembered and fearlessly engaged in the mission. Do you?

I don't know why your church is experiencing a decline in attendance. You probably don't know either. But what I do know is that it is a courageous thing to be that deacon who keeps showing up, trusting Jesus, supporting the pastor, and engaging the mission. And that kind of faithful courage may be exactly what the church needs to recapture its peculiar glory in Christ's kingdom—reaching the lost, discipling believers, and sending out missionaries to your neighborhoods and the nations.

"Get Close: Developing Deep Relationships in the Church"

I want to be a faithful husband like Ray, a loving father like Dustin, and a devoted community leader like Carl. I want to be a prayer warrior like Hilda, a relentless student of the Word like Joe, and an everyday evangelist like Matt. I want to be an uninhibited worshipper like Sandy, a selfless servant like Manuel, and an authentic friend like Jonathan. Through the years, God has used these men and women to impress something good on my soul. Their very presence in my life has given shape to who I am. That kind of impression could never have been possible from far away. These men and women enrich my life because I have known them up-close.

Christianity is an up-close faith.

Vanessa and I married when we were both eighteen years old, and we were already neck-deep in vocational ministry. We had our first son eighteen months later. As the chapters of our story were being written, we came to depend heavily on relationships in the local churches we served. We never lived anywhere close to biological family while we raised our children. "You shouldn't develop close relationships inside the church," we were advised by several ministry mentors. But we quickly learned that we could not survive any other way.

Over these past twenty-three years, our story has taken us through several churches across several states. Everywhere God planted us, we let our church family into our homes and into our hearts. We made intentional moves to get to know them up close, and we have not once regretted it. Vanessa and I have learned to embrace that our story is not an isolated unit. We are part of a much larger story that God is telling in and through Christ's churches. Our story is not only enriched by the stories of others around us; it is intentionally interwoven with them. We are who we are because of them.

In *Created for Community*, Stanley Grenz puts it this way:

"Our personal stories are never isolated units. They are touched by the stories of other persons and ultimately the story of a larger people of which we are a part. ... In conversion, we reinterpret our personal story in the light of the story of the Christian community. ... Reinterpreting our story in this manner entails accepting the story of the Christian Community as our own. We are now part of *this* people; we are incorporated into *this* community."[43]

Can you be a Christian if you are physically or emotionally isolated from Christian fellowship? Sure. But you cannot enjoy the fullness of God's grace toward you there. Nor can you grow to your fullest potential or faithfully deploy the gifts and talents God has entrusted to you.

I admit, there is danger in developing up-close relationships in your church. The more you let someone in, the more likely it is that they will let you down—and you will let them down. Let's be honest. When you really get to know people, you realize they can never actually live up to your far-away expectations of them. The distant perception of perfection is always blurred as it comes into focus. The closer you get, the more real people become.

The more you develop deep relationships with brothers and sisters in your church, the more you realize that they are just like you: imperfect, imbalanced, and impaired. But there is beautiful, biblical reciprocity in the genuine Christian fellowship of brothers and sisters who accept one another's imperfections and invest their lives toward building one another up in love: "Therefore, encourage one another and build one another up" (1 Thessalonians 5:11). You can't do this from far away. You have to do it up close.

Doesn't that make sense? The Lord Jesus declared eternal truth to the gathered crowds, but he invested himself deeply into his disciples as they reclined together at the tables and walked together along the roads. Peter led the Jerusalem Council in important ecclesial decisions from his post, but he multiplied his ministry through his daily relationship with John Mark. The years Barnabas spent influencing the church in the city were formational, but his years one-on-one in the trenches with Saul fueled his greatest contribution to the kingdom of God. Paul planted churches all over the ancient near east, but he regularly mentioned, by name, the men and women who had become close to him in his life and ministry. The biblical model is one of intentional togetherness.

How are you doing with intentional togetherness?

If you have become accustomed to isolation, it may feel intimidating to consider developing deep relationships now. It might feel safe and strong to isolate your personal faith, but I assure you nothing could be more dangerous or less meaningful. You multiply your ministry—you outlive your life—when you enter someone else's space in humility, and by humility allow that someone into your space, too.

So where does it start? One step at a time. Pray that God would show you that person, or that family, to get to know up-close. And take a step. Make that phone call. Plan that dinner. Let them into your life and open your life to them. Then keep moving toward them, one step at a time. The sweet spot of genuine Christian community is wherever brothers and sisters are close and getting closer.

Church leader, you will not rise to the occasion of your life as a lone ranger. God created you for spiritual community. Their story is your story, and your story is theirs. Whether you realize it or not right now, you need deep relationships in your church. It is built into your spiritual DNA in Christ Jesus. Just think of all that God has for you in close community that you are missing in isolation. Christianity is an up-close faith. I encourage you to embrace the larger story of the Christian community as your own. Take a step toward someone in your church today. Get close, and keep getting closer.

"Honoring Your Hard-Working Pastors: How to Express Appreciation"

They took us to the parsonage first. We followed the Search Committee chairman's truck into the semicircle driveway on that one-acre lot and laid eyes on what would become our home for the next five years. It was beautiful. Bigger and nicer than any house in which we had ever planted our little family. Crews were there painting the walls and fixing some minor wear-and-tear. Vanessa was sold at first glance. And when Momma's happy, well, you know.

Next, we followed the truck a half mile down the road to see the church building. Imagine our confusion when we turned underneath a rusty outdoor metal arch onto a dirt road that weaved through a country cemetery on its way to the church building. We did not even see the church building until our car's suspension muscled through the first pothole. Vanessa literally looked at me and said, "What have we gotten ourselves into?" We stopped in the church's dirt parking lot. We took note of the asbestos siding on our way into the building. One paneled wall flowed right into the next. It felt (and smelled) like we stepped back into 1954. But the Lord was pleased to call us there, and he was pleased to make the next five years the most joyful and rewarding season of our life together.

Well, except for the first six months. As the church grew and began to reach families it had never reached before, conflict stirred. Growth forced difficult decisions to relocate worship services and repurpose meeting spaces. Feelings were hurt. Relationships were strained. Power struggles proliferated. Six months in, after a late-night deacons' meeting, Vanessa and I sat on our couch in that beautiful brick parsonage, and I said the words out loud: "I'm ready to quit."

She talked me out of it, thankfully. The next four and a half years were the most meaningful and spiritually formative years of our ministry together. But I felt the weight of it all that night on our couch—like eternity was pressing in on my soul. Beneath the pressure of what felt like interminable conflict, I felt like I may have disappointed God even more than I had disappointed myself.

The weight of eternity is a professional pressure unique to the pastoral calling. The pastor "keeps watch over your soul" as one who will "give an account" (Hb 13:17). He will be called down on the floor of Heaven for how he has loved and led those entrusted to his spiritual care. There is inexpressible joy in the hard work. But there is an eternal spiritual gravity there, too. When the pastor is working hard—when he's doing it right—the weight of eternity presses in on his soul.

While God was so gracious to me that night, to put his loving exhortation in the mouth of my precious wife, I often reflect on what could have kept me from getting to that breaking point altogether. In a word, appreciation. We had every tangible thing we needed. But what my soul longed for in that season was a little encouragement and verbal affirmation from the people I was loving and leading.

What do you say to a pastor who is working hard and pushing through a difficult season? Here are three things I wish some deacon, or some church member, would have said in those first six months, as the weight of eternity gradually pressed me to my breaking point:

"Pastor, I don't understand, but I am with you." Oh, to have known that just a few were "with me." To have known that they had my back and were supportive of me, even if they did not yet understand the direction or the decisions. Honestly, I felt like all the major relational influencers were against me (some actually told me they were, directly). If I had known that just a handful were "with me," I believe it would have given me the shot of spiritual adrenaline I needed to muscle through. Being "with me" did not mean they had to be "against" anyone else. I just would have liked to know that while we worked to understand one another, there were those who were with me, and for me.

"Pastor, how can I help?" Pastors equip the saints for the work of ministry (Ep 4:12). But in those first six months, protesting my leadership, many of the doers in the church quit. Eventually, almost all of them came back around. But to lose most of our ministry workers in just a few months was a devastating blow. Vanessa and I were mowing the lawn, prepping the classrooms, cooking the meals, and literally cleaning the toilets. Oh, to have just one or two deacons ask, "How can I help?" If they would have offered to share the load, that would have been a timely expression of appreciation.

"Pastor, I believe in you." Every day, church members made it a point to express discontent. I felt like no one appreciated me and no one believed in me. Perhaps if there were just a few who would have told me, it may have encouraged my heart toward endurance. To hear those words, "I believe in you," especially through a season of conflict, would have been water to my soul.

Months later, and for the rest of my ministry there, one of those same deacons would make it a point every Sunday to find me after the service, look me in the eyes and say, "I love you, son, and I believe in you." And he meant it. His words are planted deeply in my soul, still today. Over the next several years the Lord was pleased to reconcile almost all of us. And when unity caught fire, the church exploded with evangelistic growth and meaningful ministry for the first time in her history. Some would say those first six months were necessary for building trust. But if I had my choice, I'd skip them altogether. To be appreciated—to be loved and believed in, and to know it—could have saved my soul from unnecessary turmoil.

A word of appreciation can do the same for your hard-working pastor today. Choose to appreciate him, and make sure he knows it.

"No Wood, No Fire: Extinguishing Gossip In the Church"

Growing up in South Louisiana, we rarely needed to build a fire for warmth. But on the weekends, my brothers and I would often spend all night on the sandy banks of the Comite River, catfishing. Catfishing is a waiting game above all else, and what are teenage boys to do when they're board, alone, and sitting in the dark? You guessed it. We built fires just for the simple pleasure of watching them burn. We would gather some dry weeds, a few sticks, and some washed up driftwood. We'd stack it strategically and then light it up. There's something mesmerizing about a fire in the dark. Sometimes we missed a bite because we were too busy staring mindlessly into the flames. Sometimes we played with the fire and got burned. But it always ended the same way; when there was no more driftwood close by, the fire always went out. No wood, no fire.

So is it with gossip in the church. Gossip and backbiting are ravenous flames to any congregation. It starts slow and low, then catches quickly onto dry vessels who come close. Some will intentionally gather wood to throw on the fire. Others will come near just to watch it burn. Whoever has migrated to the flames, you can be assured that when their attention is on the fires of gossip, Christians are missing all kinds of important things.

Deacons are peacekeepers in the church. They are ever ready to pour water on the fires of gossip and to remove the dry wood that might fuel it. Proverbs 26:20–21 says, "Without wood, fire goes out; without a gossip, conflict dies down. As charcoal for embers and wood for fire, so is a quarrelsome person for kindling strife." Because all churches are full of real people with real problems, gossip and backbiting are always a threat to a church's unity. Always. Whether the conflict is a sweltering charcoal or a raging wildfire, the deacon is called and equipped by God to bring peace. Churches in which the fires of gossip are constantly aflame need a deacon body that is ever attuned to the dangers of conflict and stands ready at all times to quench it.

So what is gossip, exactly? And how do I recognize it? Gossip is something told in secret that, whether true or untrue, negatively alters someone else's reputation. Usually, gossip sacrifices the reputation of another on the altar of the gossiper's own glory. "It's not gossip if it's true," you will sometimes hear. Wrong. Sometimes gossip comes in the form of maliciously spreading falsehoods or misunderstandings. But sometimes gossip is simply the theft of another's information and their right to tell it. Unless your congregation is made up of perfect people, you need to live with your turnout gear on.

Proverbs 8:8 says, "Gossip is like choice food that goes down to one's innermost being." The temptation to gossip exposes the depraved tendency of us all to elevate knowledge above wisdom. When gossip is on the menu, every one of us can naturally gravitate toward it. Such a delicacy promises both immediate gratification and lasting satisfaction; it tastes good, and it fills the belly. But the improper consumption and dissemination of knowledge is dangerous to an individual's spiritual health. A gossip wants all the power of knowing without the responsibility that accompanies it. Gossip promises a secret, indulgent satisfaction deep in our stomachs. But not all that tastes good is good for you. Those who get fat on gossip are irresponsible consumers of knowledge. And irresponsibility around a simple campfire can light up an entire forest in the blink of an eye.

Here are three things to remember while trying to extinguish gossip in the church:

1. **Remove the speck from your own eye.** Jesus said in Matthew 7:4–5 that if we are to attempt to take the speck out of our neighbor's eye, we must take the log out of our own eye first. Newsflash: both specks and logs burn. It is possible that the deacon himself may be more concerned with a smoldering charcoal in a church member's eye than he is with the flaming log in his own. It is the very definition of hypocrisy to point out the faults of others while ignoring our own faults. Before you consider dousing the campfire of another, be sure to extinguish the bonfires in your own back yard. Gossip and backbiting should never be on the lips of a deacon.

2. **Step into the conversation.** "But it's none of my business," you might protest. Yes, it is. Gossip and backbiting always threatens the unity of a congregation, and protecting unity is always your business. When you know a fire of gossip is burning and building, ignoring it is the worst thing you can do. The longer you pretend like it does not exist, the hotter it will burn and the more dangerous it will become. Step into the conversation and deliberately douse the fire with words of grace, truth, and love. Open the nozzle of Philippians 4:8's firehose to bury the flames: "Whatever is true, whatever is honorable, whatever is just, whatever is pure, whatever is lovely, whatever is commendable—if there is any moral excellence and if there is anything praiseworthy—dwell on these things." In the initial confrontation with a gossiper, redirect attention to

those things in the church that are good and lovely. Turn the fires of discontent into streams of life.

3. **Stay solution-focused.** The gossiper usually sees no solutions, only problems. In any conflict, focusing on the problem is akin to staring into a blazing fire, lost in discontent and oblivious to how God is working on the perimeter. Both danger and opportunity are brought to bear in every conflict. The gossiper leans back toward the danger, but the peacekeeper leans forward into the opportunity. Out of every unhealthy secret conversation comes the opportunity to correct false information, to biblically reprove and admonish the child of God toward spiritual growth, and to prayerfully discern the genuine concerns behind church members' words. Don't let the fire hypnotize you, deacon. Listen to the problem, but always stay focused on the solution.

Gossip is just around every corner in your congregation. But where there is no wood, there will be no fire. As peacekeepers in the church, deacons need to be on the lookout for both simmering coals and raging fires. In Matthew 7:4–5 fashion, a deacon of good character is one who lives logless so that he can help his brothers and sisters live speckless. He is a man who is ever prepared with his turnout gear on. He redirects the conversation from danger to opportunity, from problems to solutions. He douses existing flames with words of grace and truth while clearing the area of dry limbs that might be used as fuel for the fire. He extinguishes the gossip of men and, in so doing, reflects the glory of God.

"Passing the Torch: Investing in the Next Generation of Servant Leaders"

"That whole generation was also gathered to their ancestors.
After them another generation rose up who did not know the Lord
or the works He had done for Israel." (Judges 2:10)

Judges 2:10 should be every church leader's greatest fear. Joshua's generation was the generation of the conquest. These men saw the rushing waters of the Jordan River stack up, the walls of Jericho fall, and the sun stand still in the sky. The Lord had done miraculous, awe-inspiring things in the lives of these men. He had delivered on every promise. Yet somehow, the next generation knew nothing of God's faithfulness or God's power. Perhaps the men of Joshua's generation were too busy fighting kingdom battles and doing kingdom things to teach the younger men how to know and follow the Lord. Instead of the torch being passed on for the next leg of the kingdom race, it was extinguished in the hands of men who ran their whole lives to advance it.

One common mistake in a deacon body is to be so protective of (or proud of) the kingdom advance one generation has made that there is an apprehension or an unwillingness to let go of the torch. This makes for an awkward transition, indeed. Power struggle. Tension. And, ultimately, failure. Faithful deacons in every generation must be about the business of reproducing themselves in the lives of younger men. We should never be so busy fighting kingdom battles and doing kingdom things, or so proud of our kingdom wins, that we fail to invest in the next generation of servant leaders. The stakes are too high, and the cause of the message of the gospel is too important, for anything less. Your local church cannot afford for the gospel torch to be extinguished while in your hands. It must be passed down "to faithful men" (2 Tim. 2:2).

Another common mistake within a deacon body is to be so

overjoyed at the presence of young men in the church that the responsibility is passed down to quickly or too carelessly. Almost with a sense of relief from exhaustion, the torch is handed to young men with no training and no understanding of the difficulties of the race. Prayerful discernment must be employed when choosing whom to invest in for the future of the deacon ministry. The torch of servant leadership should not just be passed down to "faithful men," but to "faithful men who will be able to teach others also" (2 Tim. 2:2).

Investing in the next generation of servant leaders is a clear, biblical priority. But how do you know in whom to invest? How can you identify younger men in your congregation who will carry the torch in their own generation and then faithfully pass it down to the next? Here are four suggestions:

1. **Look for young men who are already servant leaders.** The goal is not to look for those who have the potential to serve faithfully in the future. Look for those who are serving faithfully now. Serving the membership is not unique to the deacon. Galatians 5:13 teaches that all members of the body should be actively serving one another. Deacons are not the only servants of the church. They are the *lead* servants of the church. Look for men who already understand and embody this truth, even without the title.

2. **Look for young men who are leading their own families well.** In a culture in which the fabric of family is quickly unraveling, this quality is absolutely essential. You are looking for a young man who, if married, is wholly devoted to his wife. His children (if he has children) respect him and he shows them appropriate fatherly love. As soon as a man is given a leadership position or title in the church, Satan draws a big red target on his family. The young man's home must be Christ-centered, biblically sound, and deeply rooted in loving devotion. Often, the office of deacon involves some level of management in church affairs. It is nonsensical to believe that a man who cannot manage his own children and

household well would have the spiritual competency to appropriately manage affairs of the church (1 Tim. 3:12).

3. **Look for young men who are teachable.** Only a foolish man would hate correction or refuse to "consult the wise" (Pr. 15:12). As you prayerfully look for young men in your congregation, look for those who are wise enough to admit when they are wrong and then learn from it. Look for those who do not pretend to have all the answers, but are willing to receive advice and learn from older leaders in the church.

4. **Look for young men who are mature and maturing in the faith.** Spiritual maturity is not an arrival point. It's a lifelong journey. In 1 Timothy 3:9, Paul insists that men who may be considered for the office of deacon "hold to the mystery of the faith with a clear conscience." Our culture is growing more and more hostile to sound, biblical faith. Therefore, the next generation of deacons must be able to hold firmly to the gospel when it is questioned and/or attacked in new ways.

An effective deacon ministry is always but one generation away from extinction. If your deacon body is not intentional about incubating, investing in, mentoring, and entrusting the ministry to the next generation of servant leaders, every kingdom win you have worked hard to gain will die a slow, painful death. Faithful devotion to the gospel in your generation always includes carefully passing the torch to the next. Identify the next generation of servant leaders in your church. Invest in them. And when the time is right, pass the torch.

"Pilgriming: Navigating the Crisis of Personal Transition"

O f all the New Testament writers, Peter has a rather interesting perspective on personal transition. He opens his first epistle by addressing it to the *parepidēmos* (*pilgrims*) "dispersed" throughout the ancient Near East. For Peter, Christians are in a constant state of transition. No matter where we go or how long we're there, we live with a sense that we're not quite home. Not yet, anyway. And depending on the places you pass through, at any given moment your transitory environment can evolve, sometimes rather quickly, from crazy to crisis. Let me explain.

In late 2022, my wife Vanessa and I prayerfully agreed to allow my name to be placed into consideration for an out-of-state ministry opportunity. We built lasting friendships in Texas for twenty years and honestly had not often considered moving out of state. But something was different about this opportunity. From the first interview through the final decision, we knew God was in it. March 20, after months of interviews, praying, and traveling back and forth, the South Carolina Baptist Convention voted unanimously to call me as their next Executive Director-Treasurer. Praise the Lord!

At the time of my writing, that was twelve days ago. And if I thought the three months of candidacy was crazy, these last two weeks we have just about been in full-on crisis mode. I can deal with crazy. But to be honest, when crazy turns to crisis it really stretches me. I like things orderly, planned, and unsurprising. But major life transition doesn't work that way. You know the drill. We need to sell our house, buy a house, and let our son finish the semester in Fort Worth while trying to find a school for him to attend in South Carolina this Fall. We're packing up our lives and moving 1,000 miles away from every friendship we've developed these last twenty years. I'm back and forth to South Carolina every week right now, working there and living here. I woke up this morning and literally forgot what state I was in. I told Vanessa on the phone that the next two months are going to test and stretch us more than we have imagined.

When personal transitions come our way, it is amazing how quickly crazy-mode can turn to crisis-mode. No Christian is exempt from the crisis of transition, because our very calling in Christ is a calling to transition. We shouldn't feel "at home" here. We are *parepidēmos*. We are just passing through.

Like everyone else, deacons navigate transitional crises of many kinds: occupational, familial, health, financial, etc. Allow me to share with you two daily practices Vanessa and I are re-learning as we navigate our season of transition. They are helping us keep first things first and lead from healthy souls. I pray they will help you, too, as you navigate your own transition.

Pray more than complain. For some reason, no matter how much I complain about my various transition crises, complaining doesn't solve anything. I got frustrated at one of the moving companies last week after trying to set up a quote and complained to the representative with an aggravated email. As you might imagine, my email brought no positive change to the situation. None. Go figure. It is a lesson I'm sure I should have learned by now: complaining to people does not often produce positive change. However, I am learning afresh that I have a Heavenly Father who is not just God of the big stuff; he is God of the small stuff, too. He is near to weary pilgrims: cast "your cares on him, because he cares about you" (1 Pet 5:7); "the eyes of the Lord are on the righteous, and his ears are open to their prayer" (1 Pet 3:12). Whatever transitory crisis you are facing, know that you have a Heavenly Father who is attentive to every small detail. Take your concerns to him. He cares.

Maintain a healthy daily rhythm. "Balance" is a word I do not love, but rhythm is something I can do. My everyday morning rhythm is three-fold: (1) do something for my mind, (2) do something for my soul, and (3) do something for my body. Usually I will (1) read, write, or research for a while; (2) work through my daily Bible reading and prayer; then (3) do some kind of physical workout. I find that no matter what crisis or transition I am navigating at any given moment, if I can keep my morning rhythm consistent, I can face every moment with a sense of regularity and confidence. Transition and crisis feel like a loss of control. But my morning rhythm is something I can control. When I do, I am at my best. Peter encourages faithful sojourners this way. Throughout the first two chapters, he urges them to "be sober-minded," continue in "sincere brotherly love," "abstain from sinful desires," and "conduct yourselves honorably." These are daily rhythms of obedient grace for the sojourning Christ-follower. You can't control the circumstances around you, but you can control how you face them. So, control what you can, inasmuch as you can. Maintain a healthy daily rhythm, and you will find the things you cannot control much less exasperating.

We often think of crises as moments of danger. The potential for failure or pain is ever before us. However, crises are also moments of opportunity. When we walk closely with God through the most challenging of days, we learn more of his goodness to us and more of our dependence on him. We learn how to sojourn well when we embrace our identity as *parepidēmos*, transitioning our way through life from one crisis to another, all while setting our "hope completely on the grace to be brought" to us "at the revelation of Jesus Christ." In Jesus, ours is a forward and upward hope. Nothing highlights that truth more than a daily dose of faithfulness through transitory crisis.

"Assessing the Deep Waters of Your Ministry Area"

As the pastor of a country church, one of the perks I enjoyed most was taking my sons fishing in members' stocked ponds— or "tanks," as they called them in East Texas. One afternoon, I called to ask about the possibility of taking the boys to one of our favorite spots. The owner, a deacon, said regretfully that the pond had turned over and all the fish died.

The geological details behind this phenomenon are beyond my expertise. At the most basic level, it has something to do with oxygen deficiency between summer and autumn. During summer months, the deeper waters of a pond can be oxygen deficient without much evidence on the surface. But when the autumn pond turnover comes, between its upper and lower waters, an oxygen deficiency deep down can kill all living things in a tank within a matter of hours.

Ministries in a local church can often develop a similar problem. A lack of Spirit-given life in the deep waters can lurk for a season without giving much indication on the surface. But when the waters finally mix, death becomes immanent. The only solution is to continually inject the deeper waters of your ministry area with the oxygen-rich life of the Holy Spirit.

This is the essence of revitalization. Your goal, as a ministry leader, is to catch the problems at the bottom of the pond before they rise to the top. This always starts with an honest assessment. Because the problems at the bottom are not immediately noticeable on the surface, honest assessment must be a regular habit of ministry area leaders. Allow me to give you five suggestions for assessing the deep waters of your ministry area.

1. **How does this ministry fit into the larger purpose/vision of the church?** Ministries that thrive have a clear understanding of how they fit into the larger purpose and vision of the church. Each ministry area is not a silo unto itself. Rather, it is one tributary that feeds into a much larger stream. Bottom-level questions to keep before the ministry's leadership are those that honestly evaluate how the ministry is helping the church fulfill its overall mission.

2. **What is God stirring in the lives of people serving in this ministry area?** It's a shame that no one takes the time to assess the fish in a pond until the environment has become so toxic that it kills them. The greatest resource and the greatest joy in your ministry

area will always be the people who are plugged into it. God works in and through people. So look for signs of spiritual health or spiritual illness. Promote health, and prayerfully minister through illness. Don't be so enamored by the pond itself that you neglect the fish swimming in it. Spiritually healthy ministries are made up of spiritually healthy people.

3. **Is there a clear, measurable goal for success?** If you don't know what you're looking for, you will certainly never find it. Does your team know what the win is? Have they been allowed to speak into the process for achieving it? Without an identifiable goal, there is nothing to move toward. Ministry ponds become stagnant when there is no forward direction. And stagnant ponds will eventually see death.

4. **Does the team agree on the value and direction of the ministry?** The degree to which your people understand and own the value of the ministry will be the degree to which they are invested in it. Perhaps at the next ministry team meeting, you can allow the team to speak into this. Ask open-ended questions like, "What exactly are we hoping to accomplish?" "What are some one-word values our team wants to embody as we serve?" "When we are experiencing success as a ministry team, how will that success benefit the church body and the kingdom of God at large?" "How will we know if we are not being successful?"

5. **Who am I mentoring to eventually replace me?** In the kingdom of God everyone is invaluable, but no one is indispensable. Ministries that thrive and survive are led by people who train, equip, resource, and release new leaders. You can tell that a ministry is healthy when there is an organic reproduction in the deeper waters. For one reason or another, one day you will no longer be the leader of your ministry area. Count on it. The only way the ministry will continue to thrive is if there has been new life reproduced in the deep waters. Revitalization always looks like reproduction.

Is there life in the deeper waters of your ministry? Revitalization will begin with honest assessment. Do the hard work of regularly asking the deep questions, and you may catch toxic situations at the bottom before they rise to the top.

"Standing in the Gap for the Orphan and the Widow"

"A father of the fatherless and a champion of widows is God in His holy dwelling." (Psalm 68:5)

In the first-century Near East, those with no inheritance were often ostracized; orphans had no family name to claim, and widows lost their economic value the moment they lost their husbands. They were stuck on the bottom rung of the social ladder—the outcast, the pedestrian, the indigent. But the heart of God has always been soft toward the marginalized and forgotten. Isn't it amazing that the God of the Ages would rise to be the champion of someone who is defeated by his or her very identity? Isn't it awesome that this God would add His name to the nameless and would confess His unfailing love to the unloved?

It is an indescribable honor that the New Testament deacon would be called by God to serve orphans and widows, to stand in the gap between their identity in Christ and their perceived loss of significance; between their needs and their ability to meet those needs; between their heartache and the joy of the Lord. Deacons in every local church have the opportunity to be the heart, hands, feet, and voice of Christ to widows and orphans today. Allow me to offer a few suggestions for prayer and action that every deacon can take right now toward standing in the gap for widows and orphans in your church and community.

Widows/Widowers

Prayer: Pray that they will be reminded of the immensity with which God loves them. Pray that when the enemy creeps in to wage war on their emotions concerning their value to the church and the community, they would take those thoughts captive to Christ.

Action: Find a widow or widower in your church this week and commit to personally reaching out for the simple purpose of encouragement once a week for the next month. Through phone calls, handwritten cards, and/or personal visits, remind them that they are loved and valued both by God and by the church. Be an intentional encourager.

Prayer: Pray that in every moment of grief, God will grant them the ability to remember and celebrate the good moments God gave them with their spouse. And pray that genuine joy will overshadow the sorrow that might accompany these memories.

Action: Going places they used to go together is often very difficult. The next time you see a widow or widower walk into the church gathering, make it a point to engage him or her personally and walk or sit alongside, just for the purpose of keeping company.

Prayer: Pray that the Lord will give you meaningful opportunities to connect with him or her outside of the church gathering. Pray that in those moments, God will use your presence to fill the relational void left behind from a deceased spouse.

Action: Widows and widowers spell love T-I-M-E. Take him for a drive in the country like he used to enjoy. Along with your wife, take her grocery shopping one day. Invite a widow or widower in your church to lunch at least once a month after church, driving and picking up the bill.

Orphans

Prayer: Pray by name for children in your congregation who are living in a foster home or with caregivers who are not their biological parents (even grandparents or other extended family members). Pray that they will feel loved and valued by those who care for them.

Action: Take the initiative to learn the names of an orphan or orphan siblings in your church or community. Find out if they play in the band, dance, play sports, or are involved in some other extra-curricular activity. Make plans to attend these activities and cheer them on by name.

Prayer: Pray for the caregivers of orphans in your church or community. Pray the Lord will provide all of their needs. Pray that you personally and your church may have the opportunity to be an agent of God's provision.

Action: Talk to caregivers/guardians in your church or community and find out if they have any specific needs you can meet. If the needs are great, mention the family in the next deacons' meeting and think through creative ways you or the church as a whole may be able to serve them.

Prayer: Pray for meaningful friendships to form between orphans and peers. Pray that the Heavenly Father would direct them toward a friend that sticks closer than a brother, and that their hearts would be receptive to this friendship.

Action: Talk to the children's ministry leaders (or children's minister, as is appropriate in your church context) about going the extra mile to be sure orphans are connected to other children their age without being singled out in any way.

"The Deacon's Reward"

The day we moved into the parsonage, hands and feet from all the church's demographics came to help. Young men carried dressers and headboards all by themselves. Women graciously directed the placement of boxes so that we did not have to move them to their correct rooms after everyone left. Young children helped my boys break in the new back yard, keeping them occupied as the truck was being unloaded. Older men and women offered words of encouragement and endearment, the look on their faces telling the story of grateful expectation for this new season.

Our new neighbors from across the pasture came to join the unloading party. Bro. Bob was becoming rather frail in his aging years. I would find out later that not too many years before, he and his wife Diane had donated the property on which the new parsonage sat. Bro. Bob helped us unload. And he helped us laugh. The next week, he came to get my two young sons so they could help him on a very important "fish-rescue mission." Some small bream had gotten trapped in a puddle beside his pond, after the flood waters receded the night before. He held onto my youngest son's leg and arm as he stretched across the pond and captured the bream in his free hand one by one. It did not take long for me to realize that Bro. Bob was a man highly respected in the church and the community, and for some very good reasons.

As the years passed, I sought him out regularly for counsel and encouragement. But time has a way of sneaking up on us. Knowing the younger men of the church around him were worthy, capable, and a bit more energetic, Bro. Bob graciously bowed out of his deacon responsibilities, passing the baton to the next generation. That was a tough day for us all. But we honored him well and the church gave him the title "Deacon Emeritus." Every Sunday, Bro. Bob would find me after the service, shake my hand, look me in the eye, and say, "I love you, son. And I'm proud of you."

Bro. Bob was a deacon for over three decades. He knew how to encourage and support his pastor and his pastor's family. He poured his life out in service to his church. With every breath, he led by example, served the membership, supported his pastor, and protected the peace. When I have circumnavigated our sun as many times as he, if the Lord allows, I pray the reflection of my past is full of what Bro. Bob has modeled. Faith. Grace. Truth. Love. Passion.

Forgiveness. Patience. Friendliness. Compassion.

What is the reward of a man such as Bro. Bob, who has sacrificed his life on the altar of service to the local church? As Paul writes in 1 Timothy 3:13, "For those who have served well as deacons acquire a good standing for themselves and great boldness in the faith that is in Christ Jesus." The reward of the faithful deacon is two-fold: (1) a good standing and (2) great boldness in the faith.

A Good Standing. Paul uses a word here that is unique to this passage; it's not repeated anywhere else in the New Testament. It's a reward reserved for the deacon who has served well over many years—"a good standing." Such deacons, according to the King James Version, "purchase to themselves a good degree." This good standing, this good degree, is not about a name-tag to wear on the coat jacket or a plaque to hang on the wall. It dares not put a man on a pedestal or offer him a soapbox, for such things are foreign to the faithful deacon's spiritual DNA. Instead, Bro. Bob embodied well the truth that deacons always stand tallest on their knees. A good standing is about the respect, courtesy and honor with which church members value the work and life of such a man. Those deacons who have "purchased to themselves a good degree" have not done so for the admiration or the recognition of men. But, almost ironically, their genuine humility in service to Jesus's Bride has produced for them just that—a good standing.

Great Boldness in the Faith. The more a deacon serves the church faithfully, the more he is challenged to grow up in the faith. When a man assumes a biblical office, Satan draws a big red target on his chest. He'll fire flaming arrows from every direction—long distance shots aimed right for the heart. Only one who has learned to consistently and skillfully wield the shield of faith will see those flaming darts extinguished upon contact. The deeper a man grows into "the faith that is in Christ Jesus," the more his faith will be questioned and challenged in new ways. A deacon who has been a foot soldier on the frontlines of kingdom advance for decades will not soon encounter opposition that would shake his faith in the Lord Jesus. Like Bro. Bob, he is strong. He is wise. He is secure. He is bold in the faith. The mission of gospel advance in this 21st Century warzone could use more warriors like this.

Several years ago, Bro. Bob took up residence where his citizenship has been since the day he gave his life to Jesus. All things considered, that day is much closer for all of us than we like to imagine. On that day, Bro. Bob's rewards of "a good standing" and "boldness in the faith" were added the reward of a victor's crown as he heard those words, "Well done, my good and faithful servant." Of all the things this world has to offer, none is so great as to even compare against the glory awaiting the faithful servant of Jesus's Bride.

"Today is Your Day"

It is my joy to travel the United States and sometimes around the world for training and consulting with deacons in Baptist churches. I have had the honor of meeting with one or two deacons in very small churches, handfuls in normative sized churches, and hundreds in large churches. Each deacon body wrestles through its own contextual difficulties and traditions, but overall they are made up of servants who love Jesus, love their families, and want the best for their churches. Sometimes I walk into a room that is peaceful with unified purpose. Sometimes the room is tense with internal conflict. Upon reflection, I am most confident to make the following observation: There has never been a more important day for a healthy, biblical deacon ministry than today.

In some ways, this is true of every season. The more removed the New Testament church gets from her establishment, the more critical it is for her to rediscover and return to her biblical roots. In some ways, it is true of every church; the deacon office is one of only two offices

God has established for the proper functioning of every local church. In some ways, it is true of every culture; the biblical pattern for church leadership transcends every geographic and ethnic distinction.

But perhaps it is less helpful to think generally rather than specifically. This is true of *your* church, planted in *your* local context, in *this* season; there has never been a more important day for a healthy, biblical deacon ministry than today, and today is your day.

Years ago, during my time at Southwestern Baptist Theological Seminary, I completed much research on deacon ministry. One week during seminars, I was in the library late at night and early in the morning to skim through every issue of *Deacon Magazine* that Lifeway ever published. Overarching themes of servant-minded ministry permeated each quarterly release. Articles centered on personal stories and practical applications. Reading through decades of publication, it struck me that there would never be a moment when enough has been said about the importance of deacon ministry. A healthy, biblical deacon ministry is a moving target. It is more of a journey than a destination.

And here you are today, reading articles and books on deacon ministry. No doubt you are searching for encouragement, ideas, and points of practical application. You love Jesus, love your family, and want the best for your church. But you are finding it just as difficult today to navigate the winds and waves of your ministry context as deacons have for decades—centuries, millennia—before you.

But today is your day. God has called you to it. He has equipped you for it. He has commissioned you in it. God did not make a mistake when He put you in your ministry context for this pivotal season in your church's life. Yesterday was someone else's day, but today is yours. What will you do with it? Allow me to make three suggestions.

First, be a deacon body, not a deacon board.

Deacon *boards* make decisions for other people to follow. They believe their role is to protect organizational continuity from unwanted changes. Sometimes they see themselves as elected officials in a representative democracy. You will be hard-pressed to find any of these in Scripture, pertaining to a deacon's role.

Conversely, deacon *bodies* give their lives in selfless service to the church family. They embrace their role to follow and enhance the leadership of the pastor through necessary change. They each serve the whole church family, not factions within it. In a cultural context of selfish consumerism, today is the day for deacon ministries to turn away from organizational power plays and back to their biblical roots in selfless service.

Second, be relentlessly optimistic.

Most deacons I have met operate from a position of cautious hesitation. They desire positive, forward movement in their church but are hesitant to be all-in. It's like leaning backward while trying to walk forward, or like swinging the bat while backing out of the box. Cautious hesitation does not do much for the kingdom. But relentless optimism will take your deacon body to the next level.

Relentless optimists are expectant in hope, and hope is a contagious thing. With just a little bit of it, an entire ministry can be reinvigorated. When your deacon ministry is built on a relentlessly optimistic, forward-leaning hope, you will see the congregation pull together and move forward like never before. In a cultural context of cautious hesitation, today is the day for deacon ministries to be relentlessly optimistic.

Finally, be the change you want to see.

Deacons who genuinely love their church family sometimes lament the slowness of positive change. "Why aren't we more evangelistic?" "Why are we so argumentative?" "Why aren't we more committed to church activities?" The power of the deacon chair is in the influence of example. The people you serve will emulate what they see in you before they comply with what they hear from you.

If you're not careful, relentless optimism can yield to crippling frustration before you even recognize what's happening. Deacons cannot force change. They cannot even push change. But they can model it. If it is change you desire in your deacon body or in your church body, don't just talk about it. Be it. Be the change you want to see. In a cultural context deprived of Christian commitment, today is the day for deacons to model the change they want to see in the church.

You are surrounded by a great cloud of witnesses. Deacons from generations past are cheering you on from the sidelines of glory. They were faithful in their time. But this is your time. There has never been a more important day for a healthy, biblical deacon ministry than today. And today is your day.

"Trust Rides on the Back of Healthy Relationship"

Kevan Chandler of Fort Wayne, Indiana was born with a degenerative disease that left him wheelchair bound from the age of four. But at the age of thirty-two, in the summer of 2016 with no wheelchair and without the use of his arms or legs, Kevan traveled the world to some of the most coveted tourist destinations on the planet, including a few extremely difficult places to access even for the most capable of adventure-seekers. How? He rode on the backs of his friends. Literally. Three friends carried Kevan in a backpack to places he never thought he would go. Fragile as his body was, he had to place complete trust in these friends. One slip and it could have cost him his life. Returning from the long journey, Keven became an inspiration to many all over the world when he accomplished the impossible by literally riding on the back of healthy relationships.

One of the most overlooked phrases in Acts 6, which I believe lays the foundation for the New Testament office of deacon, is in verse 5: "This proposal *pleased the whole company. So they chose ...*" (emphasis added). By that point there were thousands of Christ-followers in the "whole company." We often highlight this verse to emphasize congregational government in the deacon-selection process, and rightfully so. But it's more than that. Out of thousands of church members, how would the disciples know whom to choose unless these were men they knew they could trust—men "of good reputation, full of the Holy Spirit and wisdom" (Acts 6:3); men "worthy of respect, not hypocritical ... blameless ... managing their children and their households competently" (1 Tim. 3:8–12).

You don't get to know these things about someone unless you have a meaningful relationship with them. And you don't build meaningful relationships with people unless they let you in. It's not just knowing someone that sheds light on who they really are. It's knowing them up close, for a while. Healthy, up-close relationships, over time, build the kind of trust needed to serve each other selflessly and accomplish great things together. And that kind of relational connection doesn't happen on accident. It happens on purpose.

Deacons are at their best when they are relational servants. They build relationships with the people over time, earning their trust and spurring them on to Christlikeness through a healthy combination of relational acumen, biblical wisdom and selfless servitude. To serve someone as a deacon you need to earn and retain their trust, and trust always rides on the back of healthy relationship.

For the early church, fellowship was something they possessed more than it was something they did. It was something to which they were devoted (Acts 2:42), into which they were called (1 Corinthians 1:9), and by which they were distinguished (2 Corinthians 6:14). It was a special relationship marked by the empowerment of the Holy Spirit (Philippians 2:1), the mission of the gospel (1:5), and togetherness through suffering (3:10). They trusted one another because they were devoted to one another. They were devoted to one another because they were devoted to Christ. The currency of their

Christian devotion was relationship—to Jesus and to each other.

The same should be true today. The currency of Christian devotion is relationship—to Jesus and to each other. Jesus said it like this, "This is how they will know you are my disciples: by your love for one another" (John 13:35). Christlike love reveals itself through active, selfless service. Love breaks down walls and builds bridges to healthy, God-honoring relationships. And deacons lead the way. If the people are to trust their deacons, then deacons need to be conscientious about cultivating and nurturing healthy relationships.

1) **Pray for them regularly, by name.** The more you pray for your people by name, the more God forms your heart for their spiritual, emotional, physical, and familial good. Perhaps E.M. Bounds wrote it best: "Talking to men for God is a great thing, but talking to God for men is greater still. He will never talk well ... to men for God who has not learned well how to talk to God for men" (E.M. Bounds, *Power through Prayer*).

2) **Invite them into your home.** Before deacon selection day, the early church met daily in each other's homes (Acts 2:46). No doubt it was there, in the home, that meaningful relationships were forged. Connecting with your church members at the church building and recognizing them in public make significant deposits of relational currency. But there's just something special about building relationships in the home. Be like Deacon Philip who set the bar high not only for evangelistic engagement in Acts 8, but also for servant-hearted hospitality in Acts 20.

3) **Learn their family members' names.** There are few things your church members are more proud of, and possibly more concerned over, than their family members: children, spouses, grandchildren, or parents. Learning the names and specific interests/concerns of family members is a great way to make relational deposits. Try writing those names on note cards and praying for them as you pray for the church member. When you talk to the church member,

ask about those family members by name and according to the specific prayer requests you have already been taking to the Father.

4) **Be a friend, not just a church official.** A deacon told me one time that he knocked on the door of a church member and the member answered with, "Oh no. What's wrong?" Surely church members should be overjoyed to see a deacon at the door. He should bring good cheer, a warm smile, and genuine fellowship with him. Don't just show up when something is wrong. Be a friend, not just a church official.

5) **Let them into your life.** When you earn a measure of trust, walls will come down and people will share details with you about their life and their concerns. If you reciprocate (prudently and appropriately of course), the relationship will deepen even more. Don't just be the guy with all the answers. Be the guy who's working through some questions of your own, too. People don't relate to perfection; they relate to authenticity.

Imagine the places your church could go on the backs of healthy, trusting relationships between church members and church officers. Christianity is necessarily communal. Real community is necessarily relational. Deacon, be conscientious about cultivating and nurturing healthy relationships with people and watch how God will multiply these investments to his glory.

"Four Guiding Principles for Navigating Crisis"

In the Spring of 2020, a global pandemic shut down the whole world for three months. No one expected it. No one was ready for it. No one saw it coming. Not even the church. Most churches were scrambling to discover new ways to minister to their congregations and communities. But like every crisis, COVID-19 presented more of an opportunity than a threat.

Jesus's church has always thrived through seasons of crisis. The COVID-19 pandemic gave local churches the opportunity to rediscover their purpose, streamline their mission, and mobilize servant-hearted Christ followers in new ways for gospel advance.

Perhaps you have lived long enough to see your local church advance the cause of Christ through several crises: the Great Recession, 9/11, the Housing Crisis, hurricanes or tornadoes, fires and floods, pastoral transitions, and untimely deaths. Because we live in a world that is deeply and desperately scarred by the effects of sin, crisis is built into the human experience. But God calls his servants to "redeem the time" (Eph. 5:16).

Deacons can lead the way through every season of difficulty for the advancement of the gospel and the good of the church. Here are four guiding principles that should help:

1) **Flexibility is key.** In crisis, information often changes at the drop of a hat. When information changes, plans usually change as well. As a rule of thumb, when navigating crisis, methods may be worth dating but only the mission is worth marrying. Methods may change from week to week until your church finds a new rhythm. That's okay. The mission always stays the same. You can help your congregation navigate seasons of crisis if you remain flexible through vacillating methods and strategies, trusting the church leadership and communicating changes of plans positively within your circles of influence.

2) **Innovation is your friend.** "We've never done it that way before." These are the seven last words of most dying churches. For 2,000 years, Jesus's church has been innovating new ways to advance the gospel and accomplish the mission. Don't balk at innovation in seasons of crisis. Often, the innovations that rise to the top through crisis needed to surface a long time ago. Crisis provides the opportunity for change that has been long overdue. So be open to new ideas, technological advances, and innovative methods that can launch your church into a new era of Great Commission effectiveness.

3) **People are the ministry.** The budget, the programs, the building, the schedule—none of these things are the ministry. People are the ministry. When your people get frustrated over the complications that crisis brings, remember to love them with the heart of Jesus and speak to them with the voice of Jesus. You are there for them—to serve them, to love them, and to shepherd them. Don't let the frustration of the season rob you of the joy you have been given in serving the people of your church with a Christlike attitude.

4) **The gospel is the win.** How will you know if you have navigated the season of crisis successfully? If more people are hearing the gospel than before, you are winning. If some are responding favorably to the gospel, following through with baptism and discipleship, you are winning. The biblical mandate—to take the gospel to your community and to the nations—does not change through seasons of crisis. Numbers of meals served, houses mudded out, families assisted, and first responders appreciated are great metrics for community engagement. But the greatest metric for success in church life is faithfulness to share the gospel and invite people to respond in repentance and faith. Look for opportunities to share the gospel. Encourage church members to do the same. The gospel is the win.

If you walk closely with Jesus through seasons of crisis, you might just see how what Satan has meant for evil, God can use for good. He is still in this business today, as his faithful servants commit to redeeming the time. So let these four principles guide you through your next season of crisis. Flexibility is key. Innovation is your friend. People are the ministry. The gospel is the win.

Notes

1 Matt Smethurst, *Deacons: How They Serve and Strengthen the Church* (Wheaton, IL: Crossway), 44.

2 Smethurst, *Deacons*, 56.

3 Baptist Faith and Message 2000, Article VI "The Church," https://bfm.sbc.net/bfm2000/.

4 Peter F. Drucker, *Managing for the Future: The 1990s and Beyond* (New York: Truman Talley Books / Plume Publishers, 1992), 122.

5 Tony Wolfe, "Deacons At Work: 5 Biblical Wats to Be on Mission in the Workplace," in *Deacon Magazine Vol. 49. no. 3* (Nashville: Lifeway Christian Resources, Spring 2019) pp.19-20.

6 Howard B. Foshee, *Now That You're a Deacon* (Nashville: B&H Publishing, 1975), 13.

7 Tony Wolfe, "Get Closer: A Call to Develop Deeper Relationships in Your Church Family," in *Deacon Magazine* Vol. 53 no. 3 (Nashville: Lifeway Christian Resources, Spring 2023), 37-39.

8 Wolfe, "Get Closer," 39.

9 Foshee, *Now That You're A Deacon*, 51.

10 Tony Wolfe, "Passing the Torch: Investing in the Next Generation of Servant Leaders," in *Deacon Magazine* Vol. 49 no. 1 (Nashville: Lifeway Christian Resources, Fall 2018), 22-24.

11 Foshee, *Now that You're a Deacon*, 46-47.

12 Aubrey Malphurs, *Being Leaders: The Nature of Authentic Christian Leadership* (Grand Rapids: Baker Books, 2003), 42.

13 Bob Smietana, "Research: Unchurched will talk about faith, not interested in going to church," June 28, 2016 (https://news.lifeway.com/2016/06/28/research-unchurched-will-talk-about-faith-not-interested-in-going-to-church/).

14 Tony Wolfe, "Standing in the Gap for the Orphan and the Widow," in *Deacon Magazine* Vol. 50 no. 1 (Nashville: Lifeway Christian Resources, Fall 2019) 30-31.

15 Stanley Grenz, *Created For Community: Connecting Christian Belief with Christian Living* (Grand Rapids: Baker Books, 1996), 196.

16 Barna Group, "38% of U.S. Pastors Have Thought About Quitting Full-Time Ministry in the Past Year," November 16, 2021 (https://www.barna.com/research/pastors-well-being/).

17 James V. Cartwright Jr., "Acts 6 A Message for Today: An Excerpt from the First Edition of Deacon Magazine, October 1970," in *Deacon Magazine* Vol. 51 no. 1 (Nashville: Lifeway Christian Resources, Fall 2020), 35-36.

18 Matt Smethurst, *Deacons*, 47.

19 Paul R. Badgett, Alan Dodson, Todd Gray, Rick Howerton, Andy McDonald, Larry J. Purcell, Stephen C. Rice, and Alan Witham, *The Deacon Ministry Handbook: A Practical*

Guide to Servant Leadership (Brentwood, TN: B&H Publishing, 2023), 53-54.

20 Don Pucik, "How to Support Your Pastor and Staff in the Ministry You Lead: 5 Ways to Communicate Your Support," in *Deacon Magazine* Vol. 51. no. 4 (Nashville: Lifeway Christian Resources, Summer 2021), 28-29.

21 Mark Dance, "Can You Be Your Pastor's Friend: 5 Reasons Pastors May Be Reluctant to Befriend Deacons," in *Deacon Magazine* Vol. 51 no. 4 (Nashville: Lifeway Christian Resources, Summer 2021), 16-18.

22 Michael Lewis and Andy Spencer, *Lift Your Pastor: Becoming a Pastor's Advocate* (United States: Engedi Publishing LLC, 2017).

23 Badgett, et. al., *The Deacon Ministry Handbook*, 13.

24 Smethurst, *Deacons*, 52.

25 Mark Hallock, *Leading Church Revitalization: The Posture, Priorities, Practices, and Perseverance Needed for the Long Haul* (Littleton, CO: Acoma Press, 2022), p.374.

26 Hallock, *Leading Church Revitalization*, 373.

27 Steve Brown, *How to Talk So People Will Listen*, revised edition (Grand Rapids: Baker Books, 2014), 115.

28 Hallock, *Leading Church Revitalization*, 378.

29 Jim Noble, Scott Thistlethwaite, Phil Von Kaenel, and Mark Hallock, *On Being A Deacon: The Marks, Duties, and Jot of Servant-Leadership* (Littleton, CO: Acoma Press, 2019), 76.

30 Deitrich Bonhoeffer, *The Cost of Discipleship* (Chicago: Touchstone, 1995), 126-127.

31 Smethurst, *Deacons*, 135-152. I appreciate and share Smethurst's gracious conclusion on the matter: "Nevertheless, I do not wish to be dogmatic in this view, and I certainly respect the many godly believers who disagree with me. As we await that time of eternal clarity 'when the perfect comes [and] the partial will pass away' (1 Cor. 13:10), there is room for both conclusions in the kingdom of God."

32 Jim Noble, et. al., *On Being Deacons*, 13-57.

33 John Maxwell, *21 Irrefutable Laws of Leadership: Follow Them and People will Follow You* (Nashville: Thomas Nelson, 1998), 81.

34 Ken Blanchard and Philip Hodges, *Lead Like Jesus: Lessons from the Greatest Leadership Role Model of All Time* (Nashville: W Publishing Group, 2005), 55.

35 Richard J. Foster, *Celebration of Discipline: The Path to Spiritual Growth* (San Francisco: Harper One, 2018), 81.

36 Carl F. Trueman, *Strange New World* (Wheaton, IL: Crossway, 2022), 22-23.

37 Foster, *Celebration of Discipline*, (New York: HarperOne, 2018), 8.

38 Tony Wolfe, *Mile Markers: Stages of Growth Along the Journey Toward Spiritual Maturity* (Rapid City, CO: Crosslink Publishing, 2016), 108-109.

39 Tony Wolfe, "Selecting and Training Effective Deacons: Developing a Long-Term Strategy," in *Deacon Magazine* Vol. 54 no. 1 (Nashville: Lifeway Christian Resources, 2023), 13-14.

40 Smethurst, *Deacons*, 69.

41 Paul R. Badgett, et. al., *The Deacon Ministry Handbook*, 11.

42 Smethurst, *Deacons*, 69.

43 Green, Stanley J., *Created for Community: Connecting Christian Belief with Christian Living*, 2nd ed. (Grand Rapids: Baker Books, 1999), 196.